Geronimo Stilton ACADEMY

Comprehension Pawbook 3

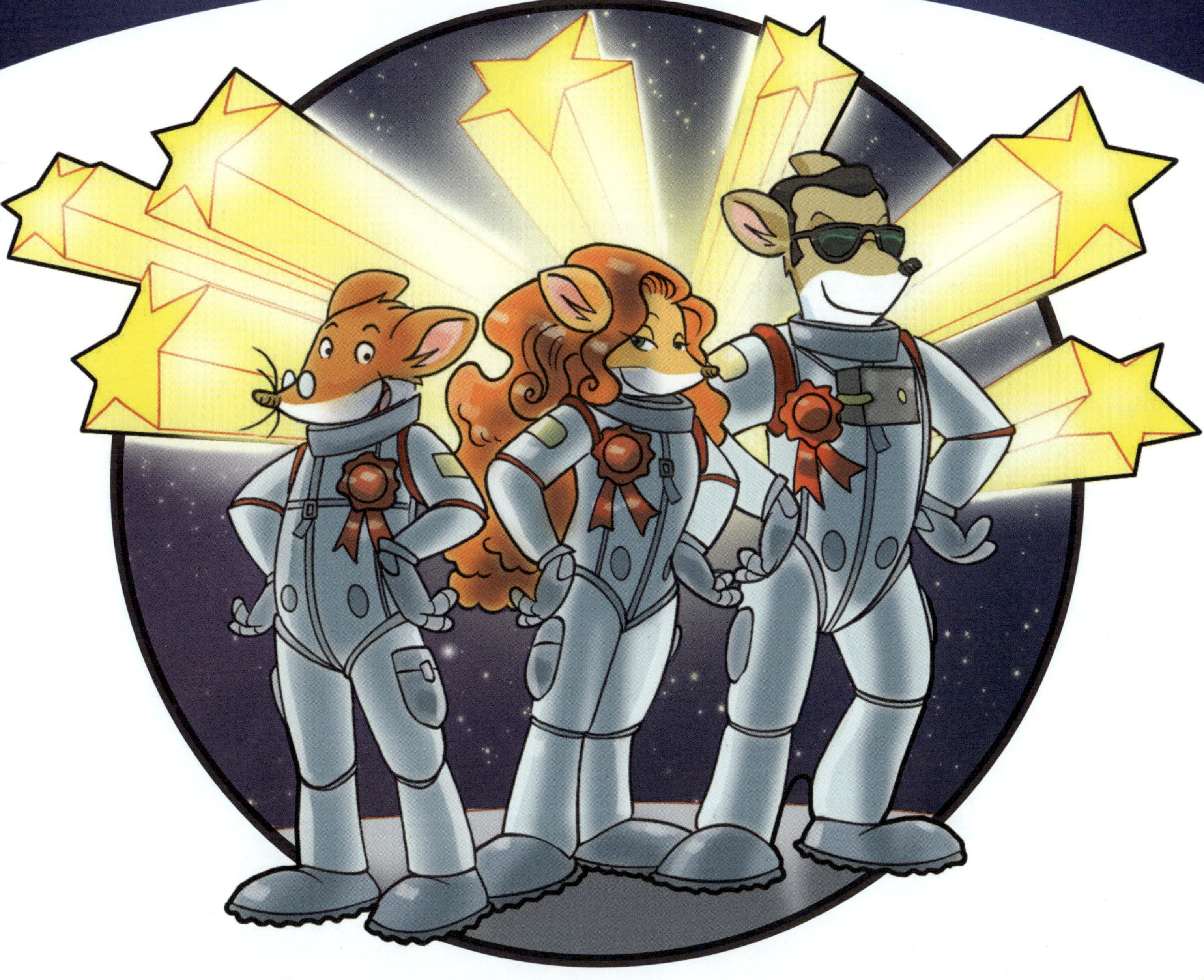

Text by Geronimo Stilton
Based on the original idea by Elisabetta Dami
Illustrations by Piemme Archives

www.geronimostilton.com

© Atlantyca S.p.A. – via Leopardi 8, 20123 Milano, Italia – foreignrights@atlantyca.it

© 2015 for this Work in English language, Scholastic Education International (Singapore) Private Limited. A division of Scholastic Inc.
SCHOLASTIC and associated logos are trademarks and/or registered trademarks of Scholastic Inc.

Visit our website: www.scholastic.com.sg

First edition 2015

ISBN 978-981-4629-65-2

Stilton is the name of a famous English cheese. It is a registered trademark of the Stilton Cheese Makers' Association. For more information go to www.stiltoncheese.com

Welcome to the
Geronimo Stilton
ACADEMY

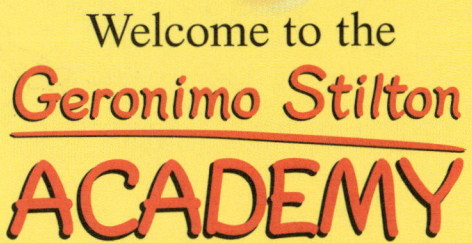

Well-loved for its humor, fascinating visuals and fun characters, the best-selling *Geronimo Stilton* series is enjoyed by children in many countries.

Research shows that learners learn better when they are engaged and motivated. The **Geronimo Stilton Academy: Comprehension Pawbook** series builds on children's interest in Geronimo Stilton. It makes learning more accessible, and increases learners' motivation to read and develop their reading comprehension skills.

The series comprises three levels:

Level 1	Level 2	Level 3
• predicting • inferring • sequencing • comparing and contrasting • recalling details and main ideas	All skills covered in Level 1 and • drawing conclusions • summarizing	All skills covered in Levels 1 and 2 and • giving reasons • stating opinions and point of view

Geronimo Stilton titles featured in this Pawbook:

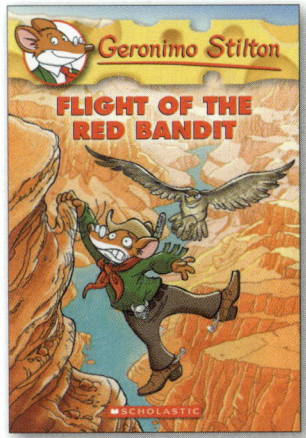

© 2015 Scholastic Education International (S) Pte Ltd   ISBN 978-981-4629-65-2

Motivating learners
Excerpts from *Geronimo Stilton* titles interest and encourage learners to read the rest of the story.

Developing comprehension skills
The 3-step format in each unit develops learners' comprehension skills and provides opportunities for independent learning.

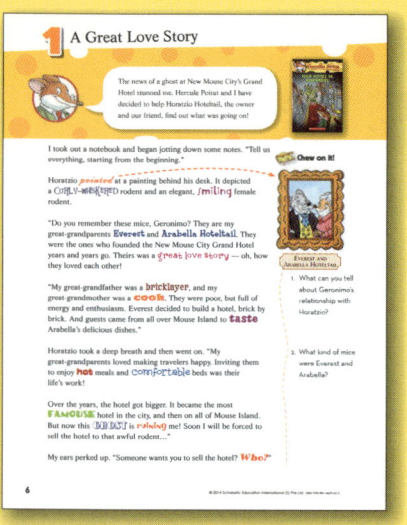

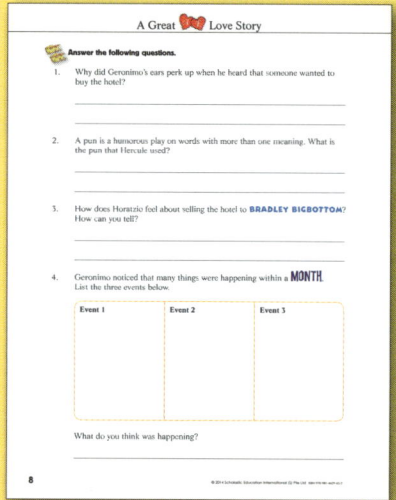

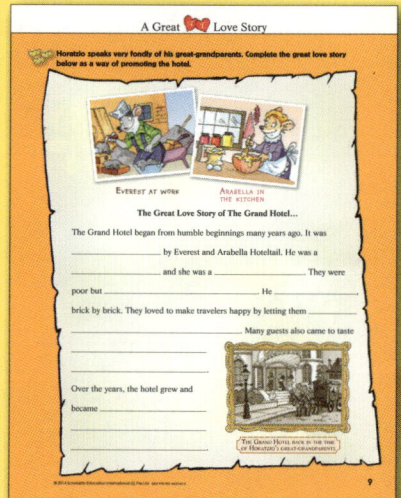

1 **Whilst-reading questions** stimulate learners to interact with the text.

2 **Comprehension questions** cover literal, inferential and higher-order reading skills for thorough understanding of the text.

3 **Graphic activities** develop learners' ability to translate what they have read and their visual text comprehension.

Extending vocabulary and understanding
Each double-page spread consists of a fun activity related to the preceding units to extend learning.

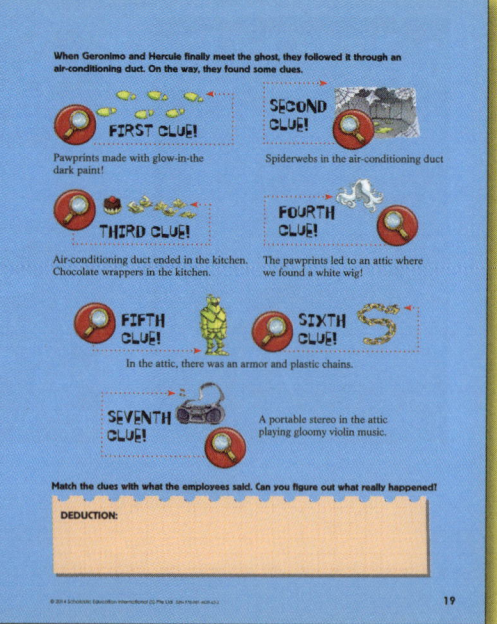

Contents

From	Unit	Title	Page
	Unit 1	A Great Love Story	6
	Unit 2	Who Saw The Ghost? Part #1	10
	Unit 3	Who Saw The Ghost? Part #2	14
	Activity 1	Gathering the Clues	18
	Unit 4	Highway Robbery!	20
	Unit 5	I Was So Excited!	24
	Unit 6	A Mysterious Shadow in The Night	28
	Activity 2	Caring for the Environment	32
	Unit 7	Three Fears and Three Surprises	34
	Unit 8	Extreme Adventure #4	38
	Unit 9	I Am The Red Bandit	42
	Activity 3	Welcome to Sedona	46
	Unit 10	Two Cheesebrains in Black Masks	48
	Unit 11	What Service!	52
	Unit 12	I'm a Hopeless Case!	56
	Activity 4	M.I.S.S.O. Secret Headquarters	60
		Answers	62

1 A Great Love Story

The news of a ghost at New Mouse City's Grand Hotel stunned me. Hercule Poirat and I have decided to help Horatzio Hoteltail, the owner and our friend, find out what was going on!

I took out a notebook and began jotting down some notes. "Tell us everything, starting from the beginning."

Horatzio *pointed* at a painting behind his desk. It depicted a CURLY-WHISKERED rodent and an elegant, smiling female rodent.

"Do you remember these mice, Geronimo? They are my great-grandparents **Everest** and **Arabella Hoteltail**. They were the ones who founded the New Mouse City Grand Hotel years and years go. Theirs was a great love story — oh, how they loved each other!

"My great-grandfather was a **bricklayer**, and my great-grandmother was a **cook**. They were poor, but full of energy and enthusiasm. Everest decided to build a hotel, brick by brick. And guests came from all over Mouse Island to **taste** Arabella's delicious dishes."

Horatzio took a deep breath and then went on. "My great-grandparents loved making travelers happy. Inviting them to enjoy **hot** meals and **comfortable** beds was their life's work!

Over the years, the hotel got bigger. It became the most **FAMOUSE** hotel in the city, and then on all of Mouse Island. But now this **GHOST** is **ruining** me! Soon I will be forced to sell the hotel to that awful rodent...."

My ears perked up. "Someone wants you to sell the hotel? *Who?*"

Chew on it!

EVEREST AND
ARABELLA HOTELTAIL

1. What can you tell about Geronimo's relationship with Horatzio?

2. What kind of mice were Everest and Arabella?

Excerpt from *This Hotel is Haunted*
(Originally published in Italy by Edizioni Piemme *Lo strano caso del Fantasma al Grand Hotel*)

© 2015 Scholastic Education International (S) Pte Ltd ISBN 978-981-4629-65-2

"A mysterious businessmouse, **BRADLEY BIGBOTTOM**. For the last month, he has been asking me to sell it to him at a **really, really low** price. And now it seems I have no choice, with this **GHOST** wandering the halls for the past month. All the guests have been complaining and fleeing the hotel! And do you know what that **slimy sewer rat** wants to do to my hotel? He wants to turn it into …

Hercule was outraged. "A toilet factory? **Never!** They'll have to flush us out of here first! Isn't that right, my dear Stilton? Did you get my little joke? **FLUSH** us out of here … get it?"

I just rolled my eyes. I was too busy thinking about what Horatzio had said to laugh at Hercule's silly pun. For a **MONTH** a **MYSTERIOUS RODENT** had been asking Horatzio to sell…. For a **MONTH** a ghost had wandered around the hotel …. For a **MONTH** all the guests had complained.

A month?
A month?
A month?

3. Why would Horatzio be forced to sell the hotel?

4. What did Geronimo think of Hercule's joke?

Excerpt from *This Hotel is Haunted*
(Originally published in Italy by Edizioni Piemme *Lo strano caso del Fantasma al Grand Hotel*)

 **Answer the following questions.**

1. Why did Geronimo's ears perk up when he heard that someone wanted to buy the hotel?

   _____

   _____

2. A pun is a humorous play on words with more than one meaning. What is the pun that Hercule used?

   _____

   _____

3. How does Horatzio feel about selling the hotel to **BRADLEY BIGBOTTOM**? How can you tell?

   _____

   _____

4. Geronimo noticed that many things were happening within a **MONTH**. List the three events below.

Event 1	Event 2	Event 3

What do you think was happening?

_____

Excerpt from *This Hotel is Haunted*
(Originally published in Italy by Edizioni Piemme *Lo strano caso del Fantasma al Grand Hotel*)

© 2015 Scholastic Education International (S) Pte Ltd ISBN 978-981-4629-65-2

A Great AE Love Story

Horatzio speaks very fondly of his great-grandparents. Complete the great love story below as a way of promoting the hotel.

EVEREST AT WORK   ARABELLA IN THE KITCHEN

The Great Love Story of The Grand Hotel…

The Grand Hotel began from humble beginnings many years ago. It was

_____**found**_____ by Everest and Arabella Hoteltail. He was a

_____**bricklayer**___ and she was a ___**cook**_____. They were

poor but __**full of energy**_____. He _____,

brick by brick. They loved to make travelers happy by letting them _____

_____. Many guests also came to taste

_____

_____.

Over the years, the hotel grew and

became _____

THE GRAND HOTEL BACK IN THE TIME OF HORATZIO'S GREAT-GRANDPARENTS

_____.

Excerpt from *This Hotel is Haunted*
(Originally published in Italy by Edizioni Piemme *Lo strano caso del Fantasma al Grand Hotel*)

We knew that some of the guests had seen the ghost in the hotel. It was time to talk to the staff of the hotel.

"We would like to talk to all the ladies and gentlemice who work at the GRAND HOTEL," Hercule announced. Horatzio answered sadly, "Please feel free to interview them — the ones who remain, that is. Many of our employees have also been SCARED AWAY by the ghost."

At the entrance to the hotel, we found OSWALD again. "What a shame to lose this precious landmark, Mr. Geronimo," he said gravely. "The Grand Hotel is the heart of our city."

"We will do everything we can to help Horatzio," I assured him. "But tell me, have you seen the GHOST?"

Oswald shook his snout, "No, he never passed by me. But many guests have described him to me — they say he GLOWS in the dark!"

I jotted down what he'd said in my notebook: GLOWS IN THE DARK.

Next we went to look for the hotel's housekeeper, MATILDA BROOMMOUSE. We checked in housekeeping headquarters, but we didn't see her anywhere — until we heard someone sobbing in the broom closet.

I kissed her paw in greeting. (I am a real gentlemouse!) "Good day, Miss Broommouse. Why are you crying?"

"I—I—I don't want to lose my job," she stammered.

"Do not worry, Miss Broommouse, we are on the case!" Hercule assured her. "Tell me, have you seen the ghost? When? And what were you doing?"

 **Chew on it!**

1. What do you think Geronimo and Hercule hoped to find out?

Oswald Rattaldo

Matilda Broommouse

2. Who was sobbing in the broom closet?

Excerpt from *This Hotel is Haunted*
(Originally published in Italy by Edizioni Piemme *Lo strano caso del Fantasma al Grand Hotel*)

© 2015 Scholastic Education International (S) Pte Ltd ISBN 978-981-4629-65-2

She **sobbed**. "I saw him coming down the stairs … Sigh… He scared all the guests away!" Then she screamed, "Look! Another **spiderweb**! Since the ghost has been here, I keep finding them all over, even if I dust every day. I do a good job, please tell **HORATZIO** that! It's not my fault the gueets keep running away."

"Calm down, dear Miss Broommouse, the hotel is in good paws! We will **save** it," Hercule responded.

In my notebook I wrote: **spiderwebs**.

Next we went to see the hotel's cook, **Sergio Creampuff**. We found him in the kitchen, seated in front of the stove. "Who would have thought that the Grand Hotel would **close** after so many years?" he sighed.

3. Why did she want Geronimo and Hercule to tell Horatzio that she does a good job?

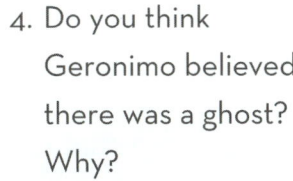

Sergio Creampuff

"Have you ever seen the **GHOST**?" I asked.

"Yes, every time a guest saw the ghost, it would also **appear** in the kitchen. It was big and tall, with **creepy** clanking armor and chains."

"I see. Have you noticed anything else **strange**?" I asked. "I mean, besides the fact that there seems to be a ghost."

4. Do you think Geronimo believed there was a ghost? Why?

The cook pulled on his whiskers thoughtfully. "Weeeelll, there *is* something, now that you mention it. For a month now, all the guests have been complaining about finding **WHITE FUR** in their soup. But no one here in the kitchen has white fur! Also, I keep finding **chocolate wrappers** on the floor, but no one in the kitchen eats chocolates."

I jotted down *big, tall, chains, white fur, chocolate wrappers.*

© 2015 Scholastic Education International (S) Pte Ltd   ISBN 978-981-4629-65-2   (Originally published in Italy by Edizioni Piemme *Lo strano caso del Fantasma al Grand Hotel*)   Excerpt from *This Hotel is Haunted*

 **Answer the following questions.**

1. What has happened to many of the employees at the hotel?

    _____

    _____

2. What did **OSWALD** think would happen to the hotel when he said "what a shame to lose this **precious** landmark"?

    _____

    _____

3. How does **OSWALD** feel about the hotel? How can you tell?

    _____

    _____

4. What was **MATILDA BROOMMOUSE** concerned about?

    _____

    _____

5. What did the cook think was strange and why? List the two examples he gave.

    a. _____

    b. _____

 Excerpt from *This Hotel is Haunted*
(Originally published in Italy by Edizioni Piemme *Lo strano caso del Fantasma al Grand Hotel*)

© 2015 Scholastic Education International (S) Pte Ltd ISBN 978-981-4629-65-2

 **Geronimo and Hercule managed to get some clues about the ghost and about the strange happenings in the hotel. Complete the list below based on what the employees have told them.**

Oswald Rattaldo

Matilda Broommouse

Sergio Creampuff

Clues About the Ghost

Appearance:

a.   The ghost glows _____.

b.   The ghost is _____.

c.   The ghost wears _____.

Strange Happenings in the Hotel:

a.   _____ appear every day, all over the hotel.

b.   Guests have been finding _____.

c.   The cook has been finding _____.

Can you draw a picture of what you think the ghost looks like?

© 2015 Scholastic Education International (S) Pte Ltd ISBN 978-981-4629-65-2

Excerpt from *This Hotel is Haunted*
(Originally published in Italy by Edizioni Piemme *Lo strano caso del Fantasma al Grand Hotel*)

We had a few more employees to talk to before we went to review our notes.

We said good-bye to Sergio and went to the hotel's basement to look for the electrician, **Jack Joltson**. We found him changing a lightbulb.

Hercule and I introduced ourselves. Jack was very happy that someone was investigating the strange situation at the *Grand Hotel*.

"Have you seen the ghost or noticed anything **STRANGE** since the **GHOST** first appeared?" I asked him.

"I haven't seen the ghost," Jack said. "But there is one thing I don't understand. Ever since the hotel started being haunted, I keep hearing eerie **violin** music. But the hotel isn't wired with a stereo system!"

I nodded and jotted what he'd said in my notebook: violin music.

Hercule winked, "This ghost is **BRAINIER** than a lab rat! But it's only a matter of time before we unmask him, right, my dear Stilton?"

Next we needed to find **CASEY VALISE**, the head bellhop. But there weren't any more guests around for him to help, and no one knew where he had gone.

We decided to go back to see Oswald. We found Casey keeping him company at the reception desk.

Casey **lit up** when he saw us. "Can I carry a bag for you, sir?"

Chew on it!

Jack Joltson

1. Why weren't there any more guests around?

CASEY VALISE

 Excerpt from *This Hotel is Haunted*
(Originally published in Italy by Edizioni Piemme *Lo strano caso del Fantasma al Grand Hotel*) ISBN 978-981-4629-65-2

I smiled warmly. "No thank you, Casey. But I would like to ask you a question. Have you seen the GHOST?"

Casey pulled out a bright plastic **ring** and began to **fiddle** with it. "I'm not sure I've seen him. But I did find this one evening. Do you think it might be a **clue**?"

2. What did Casey think the ring might be?

As I reached out to take it, I noticed that it was GLOWING. Hmmm… could it belong to the ghost?

I jotted down: plastic ring, glows in the dark.

Finally, we went to the Grand Hotel's main office to meet the hotel's director, **Ms. Bertha**. We entered a very elegant room that smelled of expensive *perfume*. I knew the scent quite well — it was the same one worn by my arch-nemesis, Sally Ratmousen, the director of *The Daily Rat*. That **odor** was enough to send a shiver down my tail.

Ms. Bertha

The room was filled with *precious objects*: embroidered silk pillows, antique furniture, paintings by famouse artists.

3. What did Geronimo think of the perfume Ms. Bertha used?

Ms Bertha was standing at her desk. She was **TALL** and a bit **stout** and dressed beautifully in a very elegant black suit. Her paws GLITTERED with jewelry.

Ms. Bertha looked at us and *sighed*. "Oh, I am so sorry that the Grand Hotel has to close!" I also heard her mumble under her breath, "Nothing lasts forever!"

4. Why do you think Ms. Bertha mumbled under her breath?

"And what will you do when the Grand Hotel closes, Ms. Bertha?" I asked her.

"Oh, a manager like me will have options, of course," she said **proudly**. "Why I've already been offered a position as director of the toilet factory … um, I mean, I will certainly find another job. With my experience, I won't have any trouble!…"

© 2015 Scholastic Education International (S) Pte Ltd   ISBN 978-981-4629-65-2   (Originally published in Italy by Edizioni Piemme *Lo strano caso del Fantasma al Grand Hotel*)

Excerpt from *This Hotel is Haunted*

Answer the following questions.

1. What did Jack think was **STRANGE** and why?

   _____

   _____

2. Why might Jack be happy that someone was investigating the situation at the hotel?

   _____

   _____

3. Do you think Hercule believes there is a ghost in the hotel? Why?

   _____

   _____

4. Why do you think Casey "**lit up**" when he saw Geronimo and Hercule?

   _____

   _____

5. What did Geronimo notice about the **ring** and what did he think about it?

   _____

   _____

 Excerpt from *This Hotel is Haunted*
(Originally published in Italy by Edizioni Piemme *Lo strano caso del Fantasma al Grand Hotel*) © 2015 Scholastic Education International (S) Pte Ltd ISBN 978-981-4629-65-2

 **Read the description of Ms. Bertha and her room, then read what she says to Geronimo and Hercule. What impression do you get about her? Complete the chart below.**

Ms. Bertha

Physical appearance:

_____

_____

_____

_____

Office decor:

_____

_____

_____

_____

What she said:

_____

_____

_____

_____

Ms. Bertha is _____

_____

_____

_____

© 2015 Scholastic Education International (S) Pte Ltd ISBN 978-981-4629-65-2

Excerpt from *This Hotel is Haunted*
(Originally published in Italy by Edizioni Piemme *Lo strano caso del Fantasma al Grand Hotel*)

17

Gathering the Clues

Geronimo and Hercule have gathered various clues to help them solve the mystery of the ghost at the Grand Hotel. Read the information they got from the employees.

Oswald Rattaldo

The guests have told me that the ghost glows in the dark.

Since the ghost has been here, I keep finding spiderwebs all over even if I dust every day!

Matilda Broommouse

Sergio Creampuff

Everytime a guest sees the ghost, it would appear in the kitchen. It was big and tall, with creepy clanking armor and chains.

All the guests have been complaining of white fur in their soup although no one here has white hair.

I keep finding chocolate wrappers in the kitchen although no one here eats chocolates!

Ever since the hotel started being haunted, I keep hearing eerie violin music although the hotel isn't wired with a stereo system.

Jack Joltson

CASEY VALISE

I found a bright plastic ring one evening and it glows in the dark.

Excerpt from *This Hotel is Haunted*
(Originally published in Italy by Edizioni Piemme *Lo strano caso del Fantasma al Grand Hotel*)

© 2015 Scholastic Education International (S) Pte Ltd   ISBN 978-981-4629-65-2

When Geronimo and Hercule finally meet the ghost, they followed it through an air-conditioning duct. On the way, they found some clues.

Pawprints made with glow-in-the dark paint!

Spiderwebs in the air-conditioning duct

Air-conditioning duct ended in the kitchen. Chocolate wrappers in the kitchen.

The pawprints led to an attic where we found a white wig!

In the attic, there was an armor and plastic chains.

A portable stereo in the attic playing gloomy violin music.

Match the clues with what the employees said. Can you figure out what really happened?

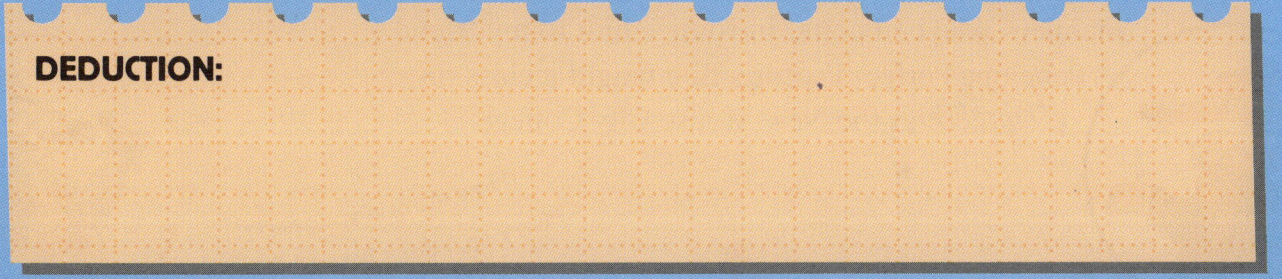

DEDUCTION:

© 2015 Scholastic Education International (S) Pte Ltd   ISBN 978-981-4629-65-2   (Originally published in Italy by Edizioni Piemme Lo strano caso del Fantasma al Grand Hotel)

Excerpt from *This Hotel is Haunted*

I invited Petunia to the Bay of Whales for a vacation, but she invited Bugsy Wugsy, her niece, so I had to bring my nephew, Benjamin. Would I still have a good vacation?

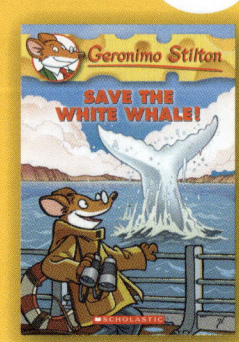

I decided to make the best of it. After all, the Bay of Whales would still be *beautiful* even if Bugsy was there. Plus, I could really use a vacation.

I picked up the phone and called **WHALES AND TAILS BY THE SEA**. I couldn't believe I remembered the number after all these years! Whales and Tails was a charming, **SPARKLING CLEAN** hotel with a fabumouse view of the bay.

It was run by a kind old lady named Miss Sweetcakes.

A **GRUFF** voice answered the phone.

"Whales and Tails! How many in your party?" the voice demanded. "Hurry up, I don't have all day!"

I was *dumbfounded*.

"Is Miss Sweetcakes there? D-d-did something happen to her?" I stammered.

The mouse huffed, "Listen, **FURBRAIN**, do you want to book a room or what? Come on, make up your mind! Time's ticking!"

What a **RUDE** mouse. He really needed to work on his phone manners. Maybe I could introduce him to my friend Penelope Perfect Posture. She taught a class on *etiquette* at the New Mouse City College.

Um...

Chew on it!

Riiing!

1. How do you think Geronimo feels about Bugsy?

2. Do you think Miss Sweetcakes still runs Whales and Tails?

"How many in your party?"
"Hurry up, I don't have all day!"

Excerpt from *Save the White Whale!*
(Originally published in Italy by Edizioni Piemme *Salviamo la Balena Bianca!*)

© 2015 Scholastic Education International (S) Pte Ltd ISBN 978-981-4629-65-2

For now I said, "My name is Geronimo Stilton and there are four of us. Two adults and two mouselets. I'd like to book this weekend. By the way, HOW MUCH is it per room?"

For some reason this made the mouse snicker. Then he asked me what kind of work I did. When I told him I was the publisher of *The Rodent's Gazette*, he let out a low whistle.

"Publisher? Of the *Gazette*?" he asked. "You must be rolling in dough! For you, every room will cost…one thousand dollars a day!"

3. Why did the mouse whistle?

My eyes POPPED out of my head. Well, OK, they didn't *really* pop out of my head, but you get the idea. I was shocked.

That was highway robbery!

Still, I didn't want to look like a cheapskate in front of Petunia, so I gulped and said, "OK."

The next day, Petunia, Bugsy, Benjamin, and I left for the beach. As we were driving, I told Petunia about how beautiful the Bay of Whales was.

But when we got there, I nearly cried. The Bay of Whales was a smelly dump! Ugly GRAY buildings crowded the coastline. And dozens of factories spewed smoke across the sky.

On the beach, papers and garbage littered the sand. And there were so many cars!

"It looks like no one has been taking care of your beautiful beach, G," Petunia fumed. "How could anyone destroy such a NATURAL WONDER?"

4. Do you think the hotel would be the same as when he went there previously?

We headed for our hotel with HEAVY hearts.

From the outside of the building, everything looked just the way I remembered it….

© 2015 Scholastic Education International (S) Pte Ltd ISBN 978-981-4629-65-2

Excerpt from *Save the White Whale!*
(Originally published in Italy by Edizioni Piemme *Salviamo la Balena Bianca!*)

 **Answer the following questions.**

1. What does "dumbfounded" mean? Why do you think Geronimo felt that way?

_____

_____

2. Do you think the mouse on the phone was **RUDE**? Why?

_____

_____

3. What did the mouse on the phone assume when Geronimo told him that he was the publisher of the *Gazette*?

_____

_____

4. Why did Geronimo call it "highway robbery"?

_____

_____

5. Why did Geronimo agree to pay $1000 for a room?

_____

_____

Whales and Tails by the Sea

Excerpt from *Save the White Whale!*
(Originally published in Italy by Edizioni Piemme *Salviamo la Balena Bianca!*)
© 2015 Scholastic Education International (S) Pte Ltd ISBN 978-981-4629-65-2

Look at the pictures below. Can you contrast the Bay of Whales in the past with the present? Complete the passage below.

The Bay of Whales was nothing like I remembered it! It used to be a

beautiful beach with clean fresh air. Now, it was a _____

dump. Instead of a pristine coastline, _____

crowded the coastline.

The once clean beach was now _____.

There used to be no cars but now _____!

The air that was once clean and fresh was so polluted because there were

_____.

What has this place become?

Excerpt from *Save the White Whale!*
(Originally published in Italy by Edizioni Piemme *Salviamo la Balena Bianca!*)

5 I Was So Excited!

Finally, we were going whale watching; but first, I wolfed down a fantastic breakfast.

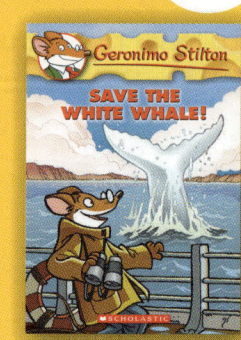

Right then, Petunia showed up. When she saw my breakfast plate, she **shook** her head.

"G, you ate too much," she scolded. "When you go on a boat, you can't **OVEREAT**."

It was too late. I was full to the brim.

A few minutes later, we boarded a **GLASS**-bottom boat. It was **amazing**! We could see the fish as if we were right in the water! The boat went out to sea so we could get a better look at some **WHALES**.

I WAS SO EXCITED!

Partly it was because we were going to see whales. But mostly it was because I had decided that as soon as we got out to open sea, I'd tell Petunia that I liked her.

My paws were **sweaty** …
My mouth was as **dry** as sand …
My whiskers **trembled** with nerves …

I was going to give Petunia a **rose**. And I had even made up a poem.

To be sure I wouldn't forget it, I wrote the poem on the palm of my **paw**.

Finally, we got to the **high seas**. The waves pushed the boat **Up** and **down**.

Petunia was below in her cabin. As I stepped down the small ladder, I felt my head spinning **around, around, around, around**….

It's because I'm so excited! I thought.
My knees were becoming **mush**.
It's because I'm so excited! I thought.

Chew on it!

1. Why do you think Petunia gave Geronimo this advice?

2. What do you think is going to happen to Geronimo?

Excerpt from *Save the White Whale!*
(Originally published in Italy by Edizioni Piemme *Salviamo la Balena Bianca!*)

© 2015 Scholastic Education International (S) Pte Ltd ISBN 978-981-4629-65-2

Then, to my HORROR, I realized something else was happening.

I wasn't excited. I was seasick!

My fur turned **green** as a cucumber. My stomach lurched.

Why hadn't I listened to Petunia's advice about overeating?

Oh, what a miserable vacation!

By the time I found Petunia, my tongue was hanging out of my mouth and I was shaking like a leaf. I felt like a circus mouse about to fly out of a cannon.

I clutched the rose (and my stomach) and tried to recite my poem. But I was feeling so awful I couldn't get anything right.

"Your fur is gray…I mean, your smile is sandy…I mean, being with you is like stormy weather.…" I stammered. What a DISASTER!

Then I remembered I had written the poem down on my paw so I wouldn't forget it. But when I looked at my paw, the ink was all SMEARED with my sweat.

Meanwhile, Petunia was staring at me as if I had three tails.

"Is there something you wanted to tell me, G?" she asked.

I took a deep breath.

"Petunia…" I began.

But the NOISE of the boat's engine MUFFLED my words.

So I tried again. "Petunia…" I began.

But the boat started to ROCK under a passing wave.

"Petunia…" I cried, before I raced out of her cabin. "I'm seasick!"

3. What kind of expression do you think Petunia had?

4. Do you think Petunia heard what Geronimo wanted to say?

Excerpt from *Save the White Whale!*
(Originally published in Italy by Edizioni Piemme *Salviamo la Balena Bianca!*)

Answer the following questions.

1. Unlike normal boats, what would a GLASS-bottom boat allow you to do?

    _____

    _____

2. When Geronimo started feeling sweaty and dizzy, what did he think it was due to?

    _____

    _____

3. What symptoms did Geronimo experience during the boat trip?

    _____

    _____

4. What do you think happened to Geronimo after he raced out of Petunia's cabin?

    _____

    _____

5. What advice would you give to anyone who was going on a boat ride?

    _____

    _____

Excerpt from *Save the White Whale!*
(Originally published in Italy by Edizioni Piemme *Salviamo la Balena Bianca!*)

© 2015 Scholastic Education International (S) Pte Ltd ISBN 978-981-4629-65-2

 **Look at the pictures below. Then, complete an account of Geronimo's experience on the boat using the phrases and pictures to help you.**

TEN STEPS OF SEASICKNESS

1 The sea is so beautiful!

2 Hmm . . . it's a little rocky!

3 Oops . . . it's really wobbly!

4 I feel a little weird. . . .

5 Yuck, I ate too much!

6 Ouch! Ouch! My stomach hurts!

7 Maybe I'll feel better like this. . . .

8 Oh, no! I'm getting dizzy!

9 I don't think I can make it!

10 Heeeeeeeeeeeeeeeeeeeeeeeeeeeeeeeelp!

The day started out with a beautiful view of the sea. It started to get

_____ and _____ and I felt myself

feeling a little _____. I regretted _____.

My stomach _____. I tried to lie down hoping I would

feel better, but then I started to get _____.

I raced to the edge of the boat…

What do you think Geronimo did then?

Excerpt from *Save the White Whale!*
(Originally published in Italy by Edizioni Piemme Salviamo la Balena Bianca!)

27

6 A Mysterious Shadow in The Night

> After the horrible boat ride, we finally returned to shore. Would I ever get a chance to tell Petunia I like her?

We **finally** returned to shore. I was so happy to be on dry land!

After dinner, I asked Petunia to take a walk on the beach with me.

I was looking forward to a nice peaceful stroll in the **moonlight**. But Bugsy insisted on tagging along. She dragged Benjamin with her.

We were only walking for a few minutes when we spotted a **Mysterious Shadow** in the night.

Was it a shipwreck?
Or an alien **SPACESHIP**?
Or a mouse-eating sea monster?

Then I heard a sound: "**Swissshhhh!**"

A shower of seawater **DRENCHED** me from the tip of my nose to the tip of my tail.

INCREDIBLE! It was a whale!

But what was a whale doing in the **middle** of the beach?

"She's probably sick, or lost her sense of direction," Petunia said. "We need to contact the marine authorities right away. They'll know how to get her back to the sea where she belongs."

Did I mention Petunia knows a lot about **ANIMALS** and **NATURE**?

Chew on it!

1. What do you think was the mysterious shadow?

2. Is it normal to see a whale in the middle of a beach?

Excerpt from *Save the White Whale!*
(Originally published in Italy by Edizioni Piemme *Salviamo la Balena Bianca!*)

Petunia grabbed her cell phone and called for **help**. While she was squeaking, I studied the whale. It didn't look good.

Then I remembered something I had heard about whales. The whale's skin is super **delicate**. It needs to be kept **moist** at all times.

I grabbed Benjamin's beach pail and filled it up with **WATER**. I poured it over the whale. The kids and I took turns racing back and forth trying to **wet** down the whale with sea water.

But the whale was **ENORMOUSE**.
Slowly, its eyes closed.
It was no long **SPRAYING**.

My heart felt like a stale lump of cheese.

"Uncle Geronimo, is it still breathing?" Benjamin gulped.

I wasn't sure. After all, this was the first whale I had ever seen up close and personal.

"Let's hope for the best," I said. I **CROSSED** my whiskers for good luck.

Just as Petunia snapped her cell phone shut, a **moonbeam** lit up the whale.

We gasped. **How incredible!**
It was a white whale!

"Oh my gosh, G!" Petunia cried. "It's an extremely rare **white** humpback whale!"

Petunia explained that the whale was white because it was an albino. Albinos have no color to their skin because their body does not produce something called melanin.

3. What do you think was happening to the whale?

4. In what way was this rare for a whale?

Excerpt from *Save the White Whale!*
(Originally published in Italy by Edizioni Piemme *Salviamo la Balena Bianca!*)

"Remember Moby Dick, the white whale in Herman Melville's story? He was an albino sperm whale," Petunia added.

I nodded.

(Do you know **HERMAN MELVILLE**? He was an amazing writer of long ago.)

I was still thinking about Herman Melville when Benjamin suggested we name our whale **HOPE**.

"Oh, G, I hope Hope makes it," Petunia whispered, **SQUEEZING** my paw tightly.

 Answer the following questions.

1. What might cause a whale to get stuck on the beach?

   _____

   _____

2. What did Geronimo realize was wrong with the whale?

   _____

   _____

3. What signs showed that the whale was not doing well?

   _____

   _____

4. When did they realize the whale was white and why only then?

   _____

   _____

5. Do you think Hope is an appropriate name for the whale? Why?

   _____

   _____

Excerpt from *Save the White Whale!*
(Originally published in Italy by Edizioni Piemme *Salviamo la Balena Bianca!*)

© 2015 Scholastic Education International (S) Pte Ltd ISBN 978-981-4629-65-2

Read the following advice on what to do when you find a beached whale. Some of the entries are wrong. Cross out the incorrect information and edit the text.

If you find a whale the beach . . .

WHAT TO DO:

1. Immediately call the authorities as they will know how to get the whale back to the sea.

2. Keep the delicate skin of the whale wet.

3. If there is sun, shade the whale so that its delicate skin doesn't burn.

4. If possible, keep the animal's tummy down with its back facing up.

5. Cover the animal's blowhole.

6. Talk loudly to frighten the animal back to sea.

7. Cover the animal's skin with sunblock lotion.

WHAT NOT TO DO:

1. Do not touch the animal (unless absolutely necessary).

2. Do not push or pull the tail or fins.

3. Do not put any sunblock lotion on the animal!

4. Don't cover the animal's blowhole. (Remember, the blowhole is the hole from which the spray exits, and how the whale breathes.)

5. Do not let any sand or water get into the blowhole.

6. Do not make any loud noise, and talk as little as possible so as not to frighten the whale.

Create your own pamphlet to tell others what to do or what not to do when you find a beached whale.

© 2015 Scholastic Education International (S) Pte Ltd ISBN 978-981-4629-65-2

Excerpt from *Save the White Whale!*
(Originally published in Italy by Edizioni Piemme *Salviamo la Balena Bianca!*)

Caring for the Environment

The Bay of Whales changed from a beautiful beach to a filthy, polluted dump because people did not care about the environment. How can you care for the environment? Take the following quiz.

How ecologically friendly are you?

Take this quiz to see if you know the best way to act to help the environment!

1 **What should you do with a magazine you don't want anymore?**

a) Throw it in a recycling bin.

b) Throw it on the ground.

c) Throw it in a dumpster.

2 **What's the most ecologically friendly way to cool your house down in the summer?**

a) Turn the air conditioner on full blast.

b) Install a ceiling fan that consumes little energy but cools the air.

c) Keep the refrigerator door open, so at least it's cool in the kitchen!

Excerpt from *Save the White Whale!*
(Originally published in Italy by Edizioni Piemme *Salviamo la Balena Bianca!*)

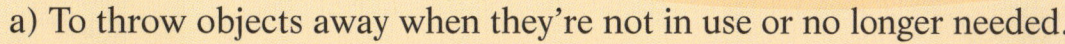

3 **To recycle means . . .**

a) To throw objects away when they're not in use or no longer needed.

b) To reuse objects so as to reduce the consumption of raw materials and minimize pollution.

c) To hide objects you no longer need in your basement.

4 **How should you clean up after a party?**

a) Throw the glass bottles, plastic plates and cups, napkins, and leftover food all into one big trash bag.

b) Hide everything under the bed!

c) Sort the trash according to type, putting glass, paper, plastics, and food leftovers in separate containers according to your city's recycling instructions.

Can you think of other ways to care for the environment? You may want to do some research online to find out how others are doing it. Make a list of four things you can do.

1 _____

2 _____

3 _____

4 _____

© 2015 Scholastic Education International (S) Pte Ltd   ISBN 978-981-4629-65-2

Excerpt from Save the White Whale!
(Originally published in Italy by Edizioni Piemme *Salviamo la Balena Bianca!*)

7 Three Fears and Three Surprises

Grandfather made me go on a trip to Sedona to look for his old friend, the Red Bandit. Not only did he send Trap with me, he told me to bring along a TINY gift which turned out to be an enormouse jar of chocolate cheese delight!

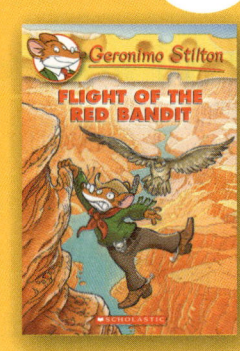

I could not let Trap ruin the TINY gift for the Red Bandit. If I wasn't watching carefully, he could gobble up all of the tasty **Chocolate Cheese Delight**! To be safe, I bought a **LOCK** for the enormouse lid of the enormouse jar.

As we checked in our luggage (including the **enormouse** jar), we heard an announcement.

"The flight to **Arizona** is now boarding at Gate Three."

And so the **LONGEST** trip ever started. We began by flying all the way from New Mouse City and across the United States to the city of Phoenix, Arizona. Trap **snored** the whole way there. It sounded like a **train engine** in my ear!

Me? I stared out the window, **worrying** about three things.

I couldn't stop thinking about the **RED BANDIT**. He sounded like a bad guy in a cowboy movie. How had he and Grandfather become **friends**? I wished that I knew more about him. All I knew was to start my search in **SEDONA**, Arizona.

I read through the **guidebook**. Sedona sounded like a **nice** little town. I especially liked the sound of the "mild climate" the book said it had. *Maybe it won't be too hard to find the Red Bandit,* I thought.

Chew on it!

1. How was Trap snoring?

FEAR NUMBER ONE:
Would Arizona be dangerous?
FEAR NUMBER TWO:
Would I be able to keep the enormouse jar from breaking before I delivered it to the Red Bandit?
FEAR NUMBER THREE:
Would I even be able to find the Red Bandit?

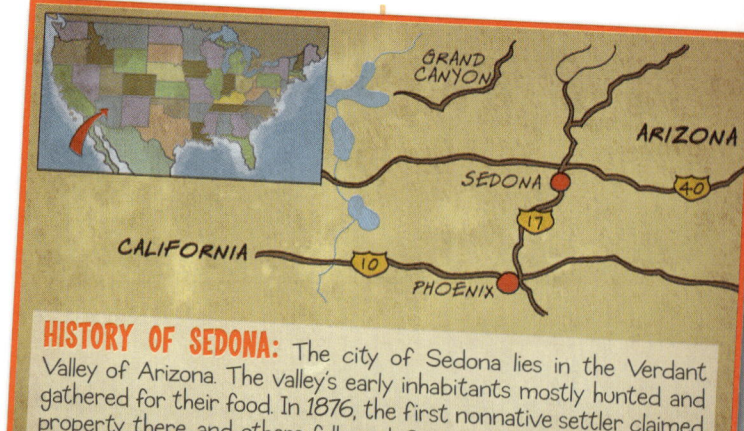

HISTORY OF SEDONA: The city of Sedona lies in the Verdant Valley of Arizona. The valley's early inhabitants mostly hunted and gathered for their food. In 1876, the first nonnative settler claimed property there, and others followed. One settler, Theodore Carlton Schnebly, established a post office there in 1902 and named it — and the town — after his wife, Sedona.

Excerpt from *Flight of the Red Bandit*
(Originally published in Italy by Edizioni Piemme *Dov'è sparito Falco Rosso?*)

© 2015 Scholastic Education International (S) Pte Ltd   ISBN 978-981-4629-65-2

Finally, the plane landed in PHOENIX. We rented a TRUCK so we could take the two-hour drive to Sedona. But of course, Trap forgot to put gas in it — so we had to stop in the middle of nowhere!

Trap and I had to hike the rest of the way. Guess who had to carry the enromouse jar!

When we got to Sedona, I had three surprises.

I had to find a way to keep the jar safe — or face Grandfather's wrath.

I tried to SHADE the enormouse jar with a HUGE patio umbrella.

Then I tried to cool it down by fanning it, but that didn't work. So I got lots and lots of ice cubes and put them on the lid.

It was no use! The spread was starting to melt! Trap began to lick his whiskers in anticipation.

"Cuz, we should eat this chocolate now. RIGHT NOW! Want me to get some bread to spread it on?" Trap asked.

"NO!"

"Crackers?"

"NO!"

"Cookies?"

"NO!"

"Okay," Trap said. "So we'll just dive in then, right?"

"No!" I YELLED, getting angry now. "NO, NO, NOOOOOOOO!" I have to give this spread to the Red Bandit or Grandfather will have my WHISKERS!"

2. What kind of mouse is Trap?

SURPRISE NUMBER ONE: Sedona wasn't a tiny settlement anymore. It had grown into a lively city of more than 10,000 inhabitants! How would I ever find the Red Bandit?

SURPRISE NUMBER TWO: In July, Sedona's "mild climate" felt more like an oven's temperature!

SURPRISE NUMBER THREE: The enormouse jar of Chocolate Cheese Delight strapped to my back was about to boil over!

Wow, it's heavy!

ENTERING SEDONA
ELEVATION 450
FOUNDED 190
AN ARIZONA MAIN STREET CIT

SEDONA: Sedona is located in the heart of Arizona, and is about 115 miles north of Phoenix. It is one of the biggest tourist attractions in the state, thanks to its natural beauty. It has a mild climate, lots of sunshine, and is home to sandstone formations known as red rocks. Visitors to Sedona enjoy outdoor activities such as hiking, biking, golf, tennis, horseback riding, and excursions in helicopters or hot-air balloons.

© 2015 Scholastic Education International (S) Pte Ltd ISBN 978-981-4629-65-2   Excerpt from *Flight of the Red Bandit* (Originally published in Italy by Edizioni Piemme *Dov'è sparito Falco Rosso?*)

Answer the following questions.

1.   List three problems that Geronimo faced at the start of this trip.

   _____

   _____

2.   Why would **RED BANDIT** sound like a bad guy in a cowboy movie?

   _____

   _____

3.   Trap began to "lick his whiskers in anticipation". What do you think he wanted to do?

   _____

   _____

4.   What were **two** surprises Geronimo had? Complete the table below to show why they were surprises.

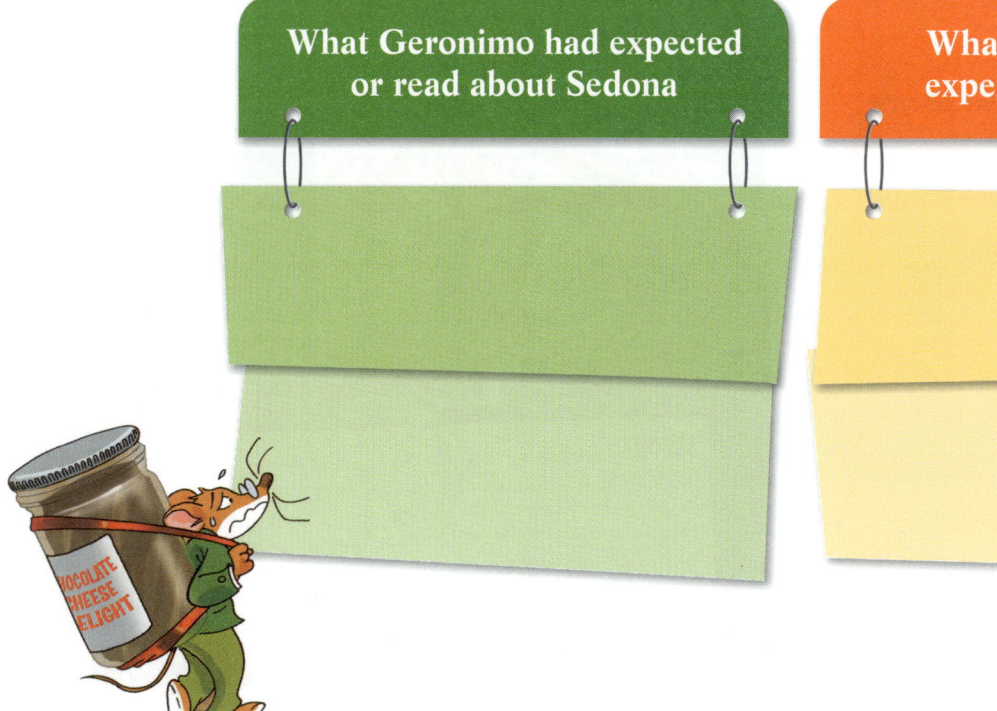
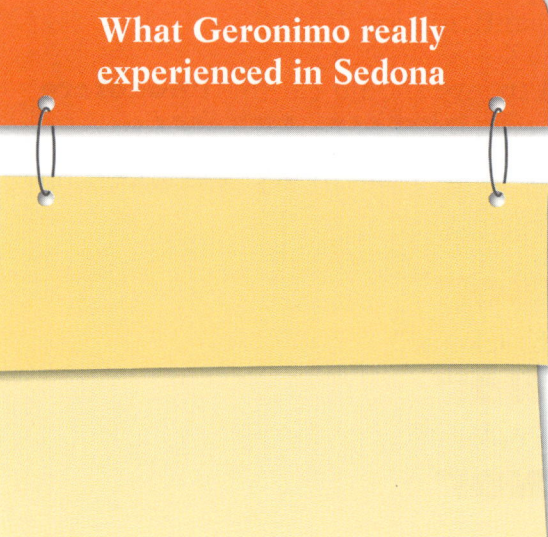

What Geronimo had expected or read about Sedona	What Geronimo really experienced in Sedona

Excerpt from *Flight of the Red Bandit*
(Originally published in Italy by Edizioni Piemme *Dov'è sparito Falco Rosso?*)

 **Geronimo tried to find ways to keep the jar of Chocolate Cheese Delight from melting. What did he try to do?**

Hmm . . .

Flap flap!

Gotta keep it cool!

Excerpt from *Flight of the Red Bandit*
(Originally published in Italy by Edizioni Piemme *Dov'è sparito Falco Rosso?*)

To find the Red Bandit, I had to go on several extreme adventures! Still I did not find him and I headed back to the adventure agency.

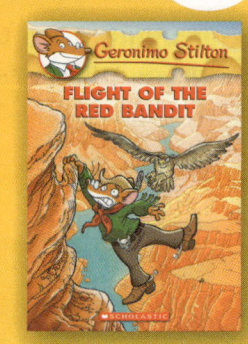

I parked myself in front of the door of the adventure agency and promptly fell asleep on the doormat. I woke up when **Poppy** opened the office.

"Tsk, tsk, Skilton," she said. "Haven't you found the **RED BANDIT**?"

Then her cell phone **rang**, and she answered. "Hello? **WHAT?** You spotted the Red Bandit? **WHERE?** At the bottom of the Grand Canyon? **Wow!** We're on our way right now!"

She **DRAGGED** me inside the office and outfitted me with a pair of khaki pants, a khaki shirt, hiking boots, and a cap with a visor to prevent the sun from **TOASTING** me like grilled cheese. Then she lathered my fur with 150 SPF **SUNSCREEN** lotion.

She drove us to a hotel, where we picked up Trap, and then we headed for the **GRAND CANYON**! (Of course, we took the enormouse jar with us.)

Trap looked happy and refreshed that morning. He wouldn't stop talking about how **comfortable** the hotel was.

"I spent the night in an *elegant* four-star hotel," Trap bragged. "I met a lovely mouse, and we dined on a **delicious** cheese soufflé in the **LUXURY** restaurant. Later a group of **FUN** rodents and I went for a midnight swim under the stars. I slept like a king in a **VERY soft** bed. When I woke up, I took a **BATH** in a tub with massaging jets. Just as my tummy was starting to rumble, room service delivered a *mouth-watering* cheese omelet right to my door. What about you, Cuz?"

Chew on it!

1. What did Poppy expect Geronimo to have done?

2. What do you think the weather was like there?

 38   Excerpt from *Flight of the Red Bandit* (Originally published in Italy by Edizioni Piemme *Dov'è sparito Falco Rosso?*)

© 2015 Scholastic Education International (S) Pte Ltd   ISBN 978-981-4629-65-2

I showed him my tail, which was still full of cactus SPIKES.

"I **rappelled** down a **mountain**…got thrown off a horse…was **Pricked** by cactus spikes…stepped in puma poo…narrowly missed a rattlesnake, scorpion, and a tarantula…**blistered** my paws walking across the desert… slept on a doormat…and skipped breakfast!"

As I was talking, the vehicle came to a stop at the edge of a STEEP cliff! I bit down on my tongue. **OUCH!**

My poor tongue swelled up. I got out and looked over the edge of the cliff.

"**WHAD ith iD?**" I asked with my swollen tongue.

"Sfilton, this is the Grand Canyon!" Poppy exclaimed. "It is one of the world's greatest natural **wonders**."

"**Beauthiful!**" I exclaimed.

Trap strapped the enormouse jar to my pack and **SHOVED** me onto the path that led to the bottom of the canyon. I turned to him, surprised.

"**Thrap, aren'd you coming?**" I asked.

He held up the hatbox. "Nope. I need to stay behind and keep an eye on Grandfather's new hat."

I wanted to **complain**, but Poppy urged me on. "Smilton, hurry up! Your next guide is waiting for you. If you move fast, you just might find the **RED BANDIT**!"

"Id's a **long** way down," I protested.

"Well, you can take the trip by mule if you want," Poppy said, "Unless you want to walk."

My poor paws were still **aching** from the night before. "I'll dake the **MULE**, pleath! Thad'll be much easier."

Boy, was I **wrong** about that!

3. What was Geronimo trying to say?

Cap with visor

Khaki pants and shirt

Hiking boots

4. How do you think Geronimo's trip by mule is going to be?

Excerpt from *Flight of the Red Bandit*
(Originally published in Italy by Edizioni Piemme *Dov'è sparito Falco Rosso?*)

 **Answer the following questions.**

1. Look at how Poppy dressed Geronimo. What kind of trip was he likely to go on?

   _____

   _____

2. How does Trap's experience differ from Geronimo's? Complete the table below.

Experience	Trap	Geronimo
Lodging		
Comfort		
Meal		

3. Why did Trap not go with Geronimo to the **GRAND CANYON**? Do you think the reason he gave was true?

   _____

   _____

4. What is your opinion of Trap? Why?

   _____

   _____

Excerpt from *Flight of the Red Bandit*
(Originally published in Italy by Edizioni Piemme *Dov'è sparito Falco Rosso?*)

© 2015 Scholastic Education International (S) Pte Ltd ISBN 978-981-4629-65-2

 **Geronimo went through some extreme adventures the day before. Look at the pictures below and his description of his adventures to Trap. Complete the text Geronimo writes about his adventures below.**

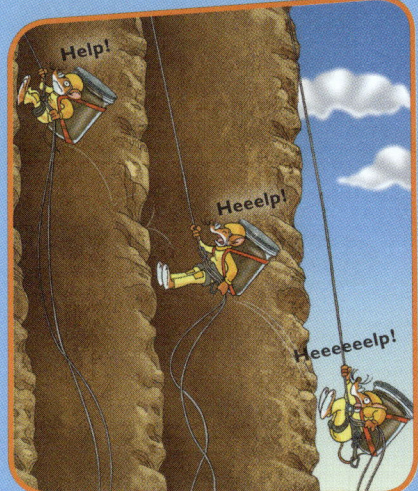

Did I have some extreme adventures!

First, I had to _____

Then, the horse I was riding bucked and reared

and threw _____

_____.

Next, I landed on a cactus and was

_____.

That really hurt! I leaped out of the cactus

patch and landed _____.
Yuck!

Just when I thought things couldn't get any worse, I narrowly missed

_____,

_____, and

a _____.

I _____
walking across the desert through the night.

Finally, I fell asleep on the doormat and even missed breakfast!

Excerpt from *Flight of the Red Bandit*
(Originally published in Italy by Edizioni Piemme *Dov'è sparito Falco Rosso?*)

9 I Am The Red Bandit

My final adventure took me on a rafting adventure down the Colorado River. Guess what? I fell in! Will I ever find the Red Bandit?

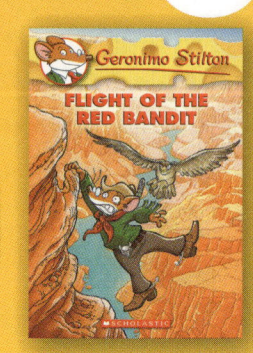

I **PLUMMETED** into the river, and the weight of the **ENORMOUSE JAR** strapped to my back sent me straight to the bottom like a stone. I'm not sure how I did it, but I managed to swim to the surface.

I *gasped* for air as the strong current **tossed** me up and down. I sank again and my mouth filled with water. I was sure my lungs would **BURST**!

PAWING with all my might, I reached the surface once more. The swift-moving **CURRENT** took me downriver with incredible speed.

The current **DRAGGED** me close to the shore. As I floated under a tree branch extending over the water, I felt a paw pluck me by the neck and haul me out of the river. A **GENTLE** voice whispered, "Don't give up!"

Then I *fainted*. When I came to, I saw two pairs of dark little eyes, as ripe as berries, staring at me curiously. Then two shrill little voices yelled, "Grandpop, he's awake!"

An elderly rodent with silver fur, a cowboy hat, and a red bandanna around his neck came closer and *smiled* at me. That's when I recognized him: It was the same rodent who'd **FISHED** me out of the river, the same one I had seen riding a horse in the valley….

It was the **RED BANDIT**!

His eyes twinkled with **amusement** under the brim of his cowboy hat.

"Welcome to my home, Geronimo," he said.

🧀 **Chew on it!**

1. Why did Geronimo's rescuer say that?

2. Who do you think the rodent was?

Excerpt from *Flight of the Red Bandit*
(Originally published in Italy by Edizioni Piemme *Dov'è sparito Falco Rosso?*)

STUNNED I opened my eyes wide and said, "How do you know who I am? Did Grandfather tell you I was coming?"

He shook his head. "Hope! He couldn't have. I don't have a phone or **eLecTriCity**."

He took a faded photo from his pocket and showed it to me.

"Your grandfather sent me this photo years ago," he said. "I recognized you right off. You haven't **changed** much."

I looked around and realized that I was inside a **LOG CABIN** — a house made entirely out of **WOOD**.

I was tucked inside a cozy bed and wrapped in a *quilt*. The quilt looked handmade out of **colorful** fabric squares. In the room, there was also a nightstand, a rug, a wooden table, a stool, a rocking chair, some small baskets, and a fireplace brightened by a warm, **CRACKLING FIRE**.

Through a small window I could see a slice of sky studded with **stars**. I realized that this house was built with love and inhabited by happy rodents.

The **RED BANDIT** nodded, as if he had heard my thoughts. "Yes, Geronimo, I built this house with my own two **paws** many years ago. I don't need a lot of stuff in order to be happy. I just want to be in touch with **nature**, and to protect it the best I can."

I nodded sleepily.

"We'll talk tomorrow, Geronimo," he said. "Have I got some **yarns** to share with you!"

I wanted to thank him, but I quickly drifted into a deep, deep sleep. I **dreamed** that Grandfather William was *nervously* pacing back and forth across my office, waiting for his new hat….

When I woke up, morning **sunlight** streamed through the window. I felt much, much better. The Red Bandit loaned me some **cowboy** clothes. To thank him, I helped out with some *chores* around the cabin, doing tasks just like they did in the days of old….

3. How do you think the Red Bandit recognized Geronimo?

4. What impression do you have of the log cabin?

Excerpt from *Flight of the Red Bandit*
(Originally published in Italy by Edizioni Piemme *Dov'è sparito Falco Rosso?*)

 **Answer the following questions.**

1. Why did Geronimo struggle to get to the surface of the water?

    _____

    _____

2. Why could Geronimo's grandfather not have contacted the **RED BANDIT**?

    _____

    _____

3. What did the **RED BANDIT** mean by "have I got some **YARNS** to share with you"?

    _____

    _____

4. What kind of person is the **RED BANDIT**? Give evidence from the text to support your answer.

Characteristic	Evidence

 © 2015 Scholastic Education International (S) Pte Ltd ISBN 978-981-4629-65-2

 Geronimo describes the log cabin as a place that is very homely and as a place where happy rodents lived. Identify the various descriptions in the passage that gave Geronimo that impression.

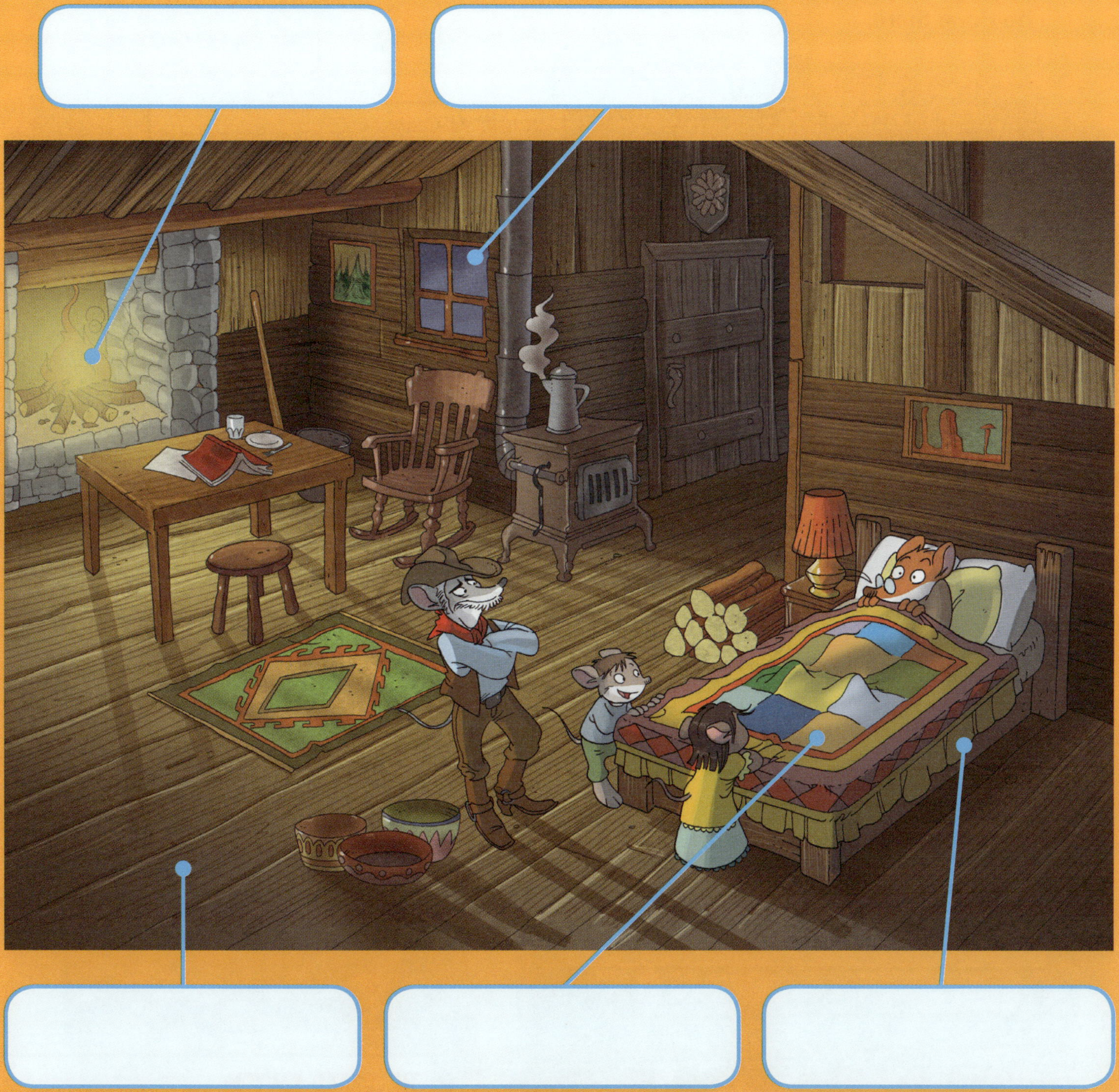

Geronimo also notices other items – a nightstand, a rug, a wooden table, a stool, a rock chair and some small baskets. Looking at how the log cabin is furnished, what impression do you get from it?

Welcome to Sedona

Look at the pictures and information given about Sedona, Arizona. Then write a short pamphlet to encourage visitors to visit the place. Include some of the activities that can be done there.

HISTORY OF SEDONA: The city of Sedona lies in the Verdant Valley of Arizona. The valley's early inhabitants mostly hunted and gathered for their food. In 1876, the first nonnative settler claimed property there, and others followed. One settler, Theodore Carlton Schnebly, established a post office there in 1902 and named it — and the town — after his wife, Sedona.

SEDONA: Sedona is located in the heart of Arizona, and is about 115 miles north of Phoenix. It is one of the biggest tourist attractions in the state, thanks to its natural beauty. It has a mild climate, lots of sunshine, and is home to sandstone formations known as red rocks. Visitors to Sedona enjoy outdoor activities such as hiking, biking, golf, tennis, horseback riding, and excursions in helicopters or hot-air balloons.

CATHEDRAL ROCK: Cathedral Rock is one of the most impressive of the red rock formations in Sedona. A steep trail leads hikers almost a mile up the side of the rock.

THE GRAND CANYON: The Grand Canyon is an immense gorge that is 277 river miles long, 18 miles wide, and 1 mile deep. It was carved by the Colorado River in the northern part of Arizona. It is managed by the Grand Canyon National Park, one of the major national parks in the United States.

Excerpt from *Flight of the Red Bandit*
(Originally published in Italy by Edizioni Piemme *Dov'è sparito Falco Rosso?*)

© 2015 Scholastic Education International (S) Pte Ltd ISBN 978-981-4629-65-2

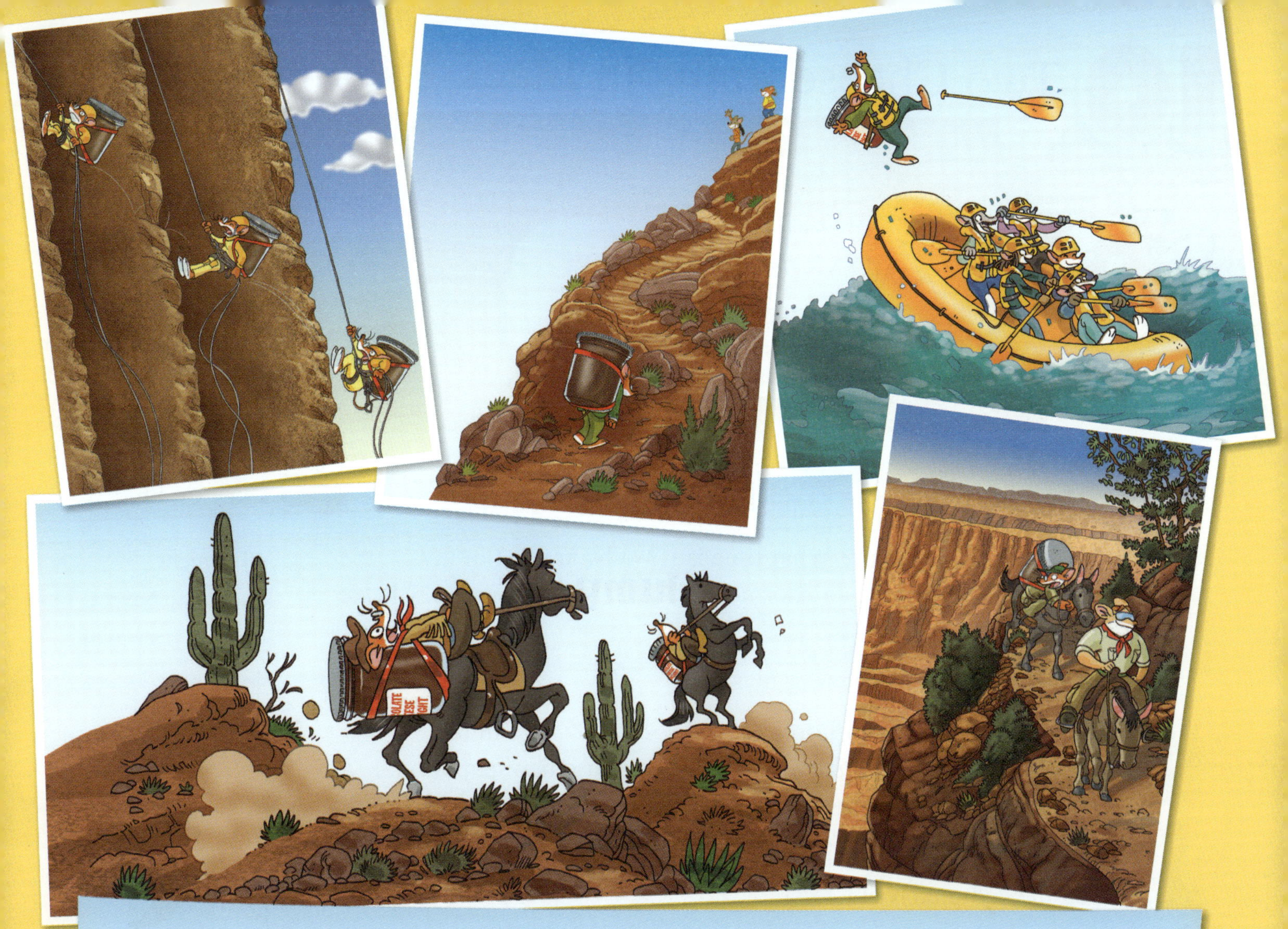

About Sedona Arizona

Attractions Around Sedona

Activities in Sedona

 ISBN 978-981-4629-65-2

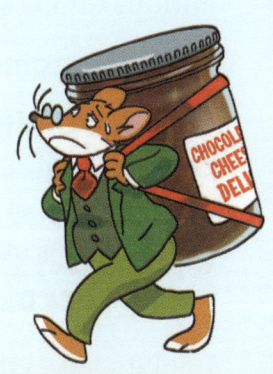

Excerpt from *Flight of the Red Bandit*
(Originally published in Italy by Edizioni Piemme *Dov'è sparito Falco Rosso?*)

My house was broken into but I managed to chase away the two cheesebrains in black masks.

With a groan I sat up. Then I rubbed my head, where an **ENORMOUSE** lump had formed.

"Who am I? Where am I? What time is it? Why aren't I in my bed? And why do I have an enormouse **lump** on my head?" I muttered.

Then I tried my best to answer myself.

"Well, um, my name is Stilton, *Geronimo Stilton*. I'm the editor of *The Rodent's Gazette*, the most famouse newspaper on Mouse Island. I'm in my house, and it's morning," I answered.

I **SIGHED** with relief. At least the **lump** on my head hadn't turned me completely clueless!

A few seconds later, everything came rushing back to me: the two shadows *sneaking* around my house the night before… grabbing my slipper… **FAINTING**. Had anything been stolen?

I ran to check on Hannibal, my **little red fish**. I gave him some of his favorite food, and he slapped his tail in greeting.

He was as *frisky* and *cheerful* as ever.

Then I checked my collection of **antique cheese rinds**. I'm very fond of them because I found each rind, one by one, in antique shops all over New Mouse City.

Not one was missing. Phew!

I began **opening** drawers and cabinets to make sure everything was where it should be. Carefully, I pawed through it all — my favorite books, my ties, a **cheddar**-colored sweater from my aunt Sweetfur, a **PAINTED** rock from my dear nephew Benjamin.

Luckily, everything was in its place.

 **Chew on it!**

1. Why might Geronimo have a lump on his head?

Enormouse lump!

Youch!

2. What can you tell about Geronimo's priorities?

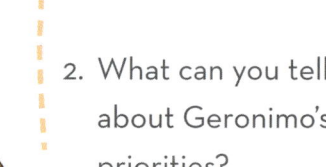

Excerpt from Mouse in Space!
(Originally published in Italy by Edizioni Piemme S.O.S. C'e un topo nello spazio!)

© 2015 Scholastic Education International (S) Pte Ltd ISBN 978-981-4629-65-2

I was so happy. The **intruders** didn't take any of the things that meant the most to me. I didn't really care about my money — but even that was all there, in my wallet, on a table in the living room.

How **odd**!

3. Why might this be odd?

If nothing was stolen, then what did those two cheesebrains in **black masks** want? Why did they run off? Suddenly it dawned on me what had happened. When I held up my slipper and **screamed**, I had scared them away!

That's right — I, *Geronimo Stilton*, biggest **SCAREDY-MOUSE** on all of Mouse Island, had sent those **rotten** cheesebrains running!

I couldn't believe it. I was a true **HERO**!

I couldn't wait to tell everyone! I **scampered** to the bathroom and began getting ready for work, happily *whistling* to myself.

I looked at myself in the mirror. Yes, I decided, I did look stronger, and prouder. In fact, you could say I looked **heroic**!

I was so busy staring at myself in the mirror that I hadn't heard the phone **ringing**. I picked up after the tenth **ring**. It was my grandfather William Shortpaws.

"**GRANDSON!** What are you doing? Why didn't you pick up the phone sooner? I refuse to be kept waiting! Get your tail in gear **PRONTO**! There were a ton of robberies in the city last night!" he **SCREECHED**.

"I know, Grandfather. Last night two cheesebrains in **black masks** broke into my house, too. But I chased them away with a slipper! Oh, and then I fainted. But still, I was a real **HERO**!" I squeaked.

Grandfather snorted.

4. Why did Grandfather snort?

"A **slipper**? Sure those slippers can be very scary. Now listen, **HERO**, get your fuzzy head out of your fairy-tale book and get moving. We need to get the scoop on those robberies for the paper. I sent your sister, Thea, over to you with **precise** instructions. You need to figure out who's behind all these robberies. After you do that, write an **ace** article and have it on my desk by tomorrow morning! Got it? **NOW MOVE IT!**" he shrieked.

© 2015 Scholastic Education International (S) Pte Ltd   ISBN 978-981-4629-65-2   *Excerpt from Mouse in Space!* (Originally published in Italy by Edizioni Piemme S.O.S. C'e un topo nello spazio!)

Answer the following questions.

1. Why did Geronimo ask himself questions and answer them?

    _____

    _____

2. What was  about the thieves?

    _____

    _____

3. How did Geronimo feel about himself when he realized that he had chased away the thieves? How can you tell?

    _____

    _____

4. Why do you think Geronimo wanted to tell Grandfather about what he did?

    _____

    _____

5. What is Grandfather's opinion of Geronimo? How can you tell?

    _____

    _____

 Excerpt from *Mouse in Space!*
(Originally published in Italy by Edizioni Piemme S.O.S. C'e un topo nello spazio!)

© 2015 Scholastic Education International (S) Pte Ltd ISBN 978-981-4629-65-2

 **How do you think Geronimo felt in the following picture? How can you tell? Give 3 clues from the text.**

1 _____

2 _____

3 _____

 **Which image of Geronimo might other characters have? How can you tell? List four clues from the text. Think about what Geronimo wants to do to impress everyone.**

1 _____

2 _____

3 _____

4 _____

© 2015 Scholastic Education International (S) Pte Ltd ISBN 978-981-4629-65-2

Excerpt from Mouse in Space!
(Originally published in Italy by Edizioni Piemme S.O.S. C'e un topo nello spazio!)

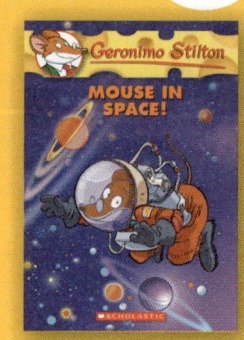

After my house got broken into, I called Safe Squeak to get them to install antitheft devices for my house. It was just the thing I needed to keep safe!

I hadn't even finished squeaking when there was a knock at my door. I opened it and saw a **TALL**, slender rodent with **long** blond fur, a dark suit, and **Mysterious** black sunglasses.

I noticed a **SAFE SQUEAK** pin on her jacket, and below it, in small print, the name **Suzy Slyrat**.

I was stunned! What service! Safe Squeak really was **FAST**!

I welcomed Suzy Slyrat and showed her into the living room. She gave me the most **mesmerizing** smile, then showed me a comprehensive catalog with the most sophisticated antitheft devices I'd ever seen.

"You were so **SMART** to call us, Mr. Stilton," she said in a soothing voice, patting my paw. "But of course, I can already tell you are a **SUPERSMART** mouse. Tonight you'll sleep like a **log**. We'll keep everything under control with our **SUPER-SATELLITE** antitheft devices. No thieves will get into your house again. And … because you're our one-thousandth customer, you will receive three pieces of equipment for the price of two!"

Done!

In less than ten minutes, Miss Slyrat convinced me to buy **everything** in the catalog — for a **FUR-RAISING** amount of money! Half-dazed, I repeated over and over again, "Of course, Miss Slyrat. Thank you, Miss Slyrat. Do what you think is best, Miss Slyrat.…"

 Chew on it!

1. Do you think Suzy Slyrat can be trusted? Why?

2. What do you think was happening to Geronimo?

Excerpt from *Mouse in Space!*
(Originally published in Italy by Edizioni Piemme S.O.S. C'e un topo nello spazio!)

For some reason I just couldn't say no to such a **CHARMING** mouse.

"You'll sleep like a **mouseling** tonight, Mr. Stilton, just you **wait** and see!" she insisted as I handed over my **ENORMOUSE** check.

When I finished signing the contract, she grabbed the paper and quickly put it away. She made a phone call, and in less than two minutes, a team of **SAFE SQUEAK** workers took over my house.

This is what they installed: **75 infrared sensors** (on the windows and doors, as well as on the cabinets and refrigerator doors!), **93 detectors** that would sense the presence of any living thing in the building, **38 CAMERAS** (at least 3 in every room!), **1 SECURITY DOOR**, **13 ELECTRIFIED SUPER-REINFORCED SHUTTERS**, and **7 huge eardrum-splitting alarms** (linked to everything).

Any mouse who wanted to get into my house now had to undergo:
- Digital pawprint recognition
- Examination of fur (color and softness incorporated with antiflea treatment)
- Measurement of tail length
- Complete examination of whiskers
- Squeak recognition

The entire system was connected via satellite to **SAFE SQUEAK** headquarters, where a system expert manned the system **24-7**.

When they left, night had fallen. I quickly wrote my article for *The Rodent's Gazette* and **emailed** it in. I advised all of New Mouse City's residents to install some sort of **ANTITHEFT DEVICE** to keep thieves away. Then, completely exhausted, I ate a **COLD** cheese sandwich and headed off to bed.

3. What do you think of the antitheft devices installed?

4. Would the system give you peace of mind?

© 2015 Scholastic Education International (S) Pte Ltd ISBN 978-981-4629-65-2

Excerpt from *Mouse in Space!*
(Originally published in Italy by Edizioni Piemme S.O.S. *C'e un topo nello spazio!*)

What  Service!

 **Answer the following questions.**

1. What do you think might be suspicious about **SAFE SQUEAK**'s service?

    _____

    _____

2. What impression do you get from the description of **Suzy Slyrat** and her name?

    _____

    _____

3. Why did **Suzy Slyrat** grab the contract quickly once Geronimo signed it?

    _____

    _____

4. What does the term "**24-7**" mean?

    _____

    _____

5. Suzy Slyrat easily convinced Geronimo to make a large purchase. List some of the tactics that she used and complete the table below.

Tactic	What she said or did
She flattered him.	
She reassured him.	
She offered a discount.	

Excerpt from *Mouse in Space!*
(Originally published in Italy by Edizioni Piemme S.O.S. C'e un topo nello spazio!)

© 2015 Scholastic Education International (S) Pte Ltd ISBN 978-981-4629-65-2

 **Look at the antitheft devices installed in Geronimo's house. Complete the picture to show what each device is for. Use the following phrases to help you.**

To sense the presence of living things in the building
Track movement
Record everything that happens everywhere
Sense vibrations near the entrance
So loud it can be heard miles away
Reliable and shatterproof to prevent entry through windows

ANTITHEFT DEVICES
INSTALLED IN GERONIMO'S HOUSE

1) **Infrared sensors**
2) **Motion and movement detectors**
3) **Video cameras**
4) **Security door**
5) **Electrified titanium super-reinforced shutters**
6) **Giant earsplitting alarms**

1) _____

_____

2) _____

_____

3) _____

_____

4) _____

_____

5) _____

_____

6) _____

_____

Excerpt from Mouse in Space!
(Originally published in Italy by Edizioni Piemme S.O.S. C'e un topo nello spazio!)

12 I'm a Hopeless Case!

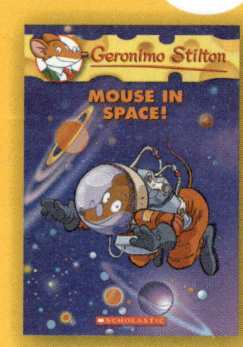

Cheese niblets! I was on a mission to find the satellite the evil mice were using to control New Mouse City. I had to be launched into space. But first, I needed to undergo some training!

The professor grabbed my sleeve and **DRAGGED** me away before I changed my mind.

"Okay, 00G, come along!" he said. "You'll be starting a **SUPER**-concentrated program of **SUPER** training to become a **SUPER** astronaut!!"

"B-but…what about them?" I stammered. "They're already trained," he explained.

And that's when the **PROBLEMS** began….

First, they gave me a medical exam. I was surrounded by a bunch of rodents in **WHITE COATS** who examined me from the top of my ears to the tip of my tail. Afterward, they shook their heads and whispered in astonishment,

"Wow … he's a **mess**!"
"Ugh … I wonder if he'll **MAKE** it!"
"Squeak … what a **disaster**!"

A doctor came bounding in the room, waving the results of my exam.

"Gentlemice, the results are clear. Agent 00G is a **complete mess**….He's a **HOPELESS CASE**!" he declared.

At that point, I tried to make a quick getaway.

"Did you hear that?" I screeched. "I'm a **HOPELESS CASE**! I don't have what it takes to be an **astronaut**! So, adios, hasta la vista, see you later, and thanks to all!"

But the professor grabbed me by the tail.

Chew on it!

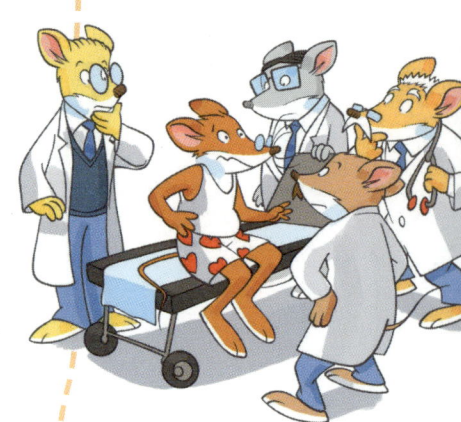

1. What did this suggest about Geronimo?

2. What was Geronimo hoping to do?

Excerpt from *Mouse in Space!*
(Originally published in Italy by Edizioni Piemme S.O.S. C'e un topo nello spazio!)

© 2015 Scholastic Education International (S) Pte Ltd ISBN 978-981-4629-65-2

"Where do you think you're going?" he said. "The chief says we have to get you in **shape** and ship you into **SPACE**! And no one argues with the chief. Don't worry, we'll fix you up!"

And, boy, did they **fix me up**! They made me swallow a gigantic pill and a protein-rich **shake**. They even gave me a vitamin injection with a huge syringe. I screamed so **loud**, they must have heard me all the way up on Mars!

Then the situation got worse: I began the **SUPER-CONCENTRATED** astronaut training. What an absolute and total disaster!

Before I started, the professor explained, "In order to become an astronaut, you must:

- be in excellent **physical shape** (and as far as physiques go, you're in bad shape!)
- have a degree in **SCIENCE** (no creative types needed in space!)
- have an excellent knowledge of **foreign languages** (and made-up languages don't count!)
- not be **afraid** of anything (and I can bet my last cheesecake that you are afraid of everything!)
- have a great capacity to **ADAPT**

Can you do all that?"

"Adapt to what?" I asked.

"Life in space, rookie!" the professor **squeaked**. "Oh, and I forgot — it usually takes **three years** to train. But unfortunately you only have **LESS THAN TWO DAYS**, so…"

"So?"

"So…"

"So, what?"

"So, you've got a right to know — you might not make it back **alive**!"

I stared into the distance until the professor **pinched** me.

3. Do you think that was news Geronimo wanted to hear?

4. How do you think Geronimo felt at this point?

© 2015 Scholastic Education International (S) Pte Ltd ISBN 978-981-4629-65-2

Excerpt from *Mouse in Space!*
(Originally published in Italy by Edizioni Piemme S.O.S. C'e un topo nello spazio!)

I'm a Hopeless 🪐 Case!

"Wake up! No **TIME** for daydreaming!" he squeaked. "You've got work to do! First you have *12 HOURS* of training in the pool with full gear with your space suit. That's to **TRY** to teach you how to move in space (though you're pretty clumsy). Then you have *12 HOURS* of parabolic flight to **TRY** to get you used to the absence of gravity (though you're already pretty slow). Then *8 HOURS* of simulated aerospace piloting to **TRY** to teach you to steer a spaceship (though you're so spastic). And that's it!"

MOVING IN SPACE
Moving in space is very different from moving on Earth because of the total absence of gravity. Before leaving Earth, astronauts perform rigorous exercises in underwater tanks to simulate the feeling of weightlessness.

Answer the following questions.

1. Why did the others not have to undergo the same training?

2. Why was a medical examination needed?

3. When Geronimo heard that he was a "**HOPELESS CASE**", how do you think he felt? Why?

4. Do you think Geronimo had the qualities the professor listed? Give reasons for your answer.

5. Do you think the Professor's assessment of Geronimo is accurate? Give reasons for your answer.

Excerpt from *Mouse in Space!* (Originally published in Italy by Edizioni Piemme S.O.S. C'e un topo nello spazio!)
© 2015 Scholastic Education International (S) Pte Ltd ISBN 978-981-4629-65-2

Look at the training that Geronimo had to undergo. Why was each stage necessary? Write down the reason Geronimo had to be trained in that way.

HERE'S MY THIRTY-TWO HOURS OF POWER TRAINING!

1. POOL TRAINING

_____

_____

_____

2. ZERO-GRAVITY TRAINING ON A PARABOLIC FLIGHT

_____

_____

_____

3. SIMULATING FLIGHT

_____

_____

_____

Excerpt from Mouse in Space!
(Originally published in Italy by Edizioni Piemme S.O.S. C'e un topo nello spazio!)

M.I.S.S.O. Secret Headquarters

Look at the M.I.S.S.O. secret headquarters. What do you think they did at each of the rooms? Imagine you are going to prepare a brief for a new agent. Complete the description of what gets done in the headquarters.

Excerpt from *Mouse in Space!*
(Originally published in Italy by Edizioni Piemme *S.O.S. C'e un topo nello spazio!*)

© 2015 Scholastic Education International (S) Pte Ltd ISBN 978-981-4629-65-2

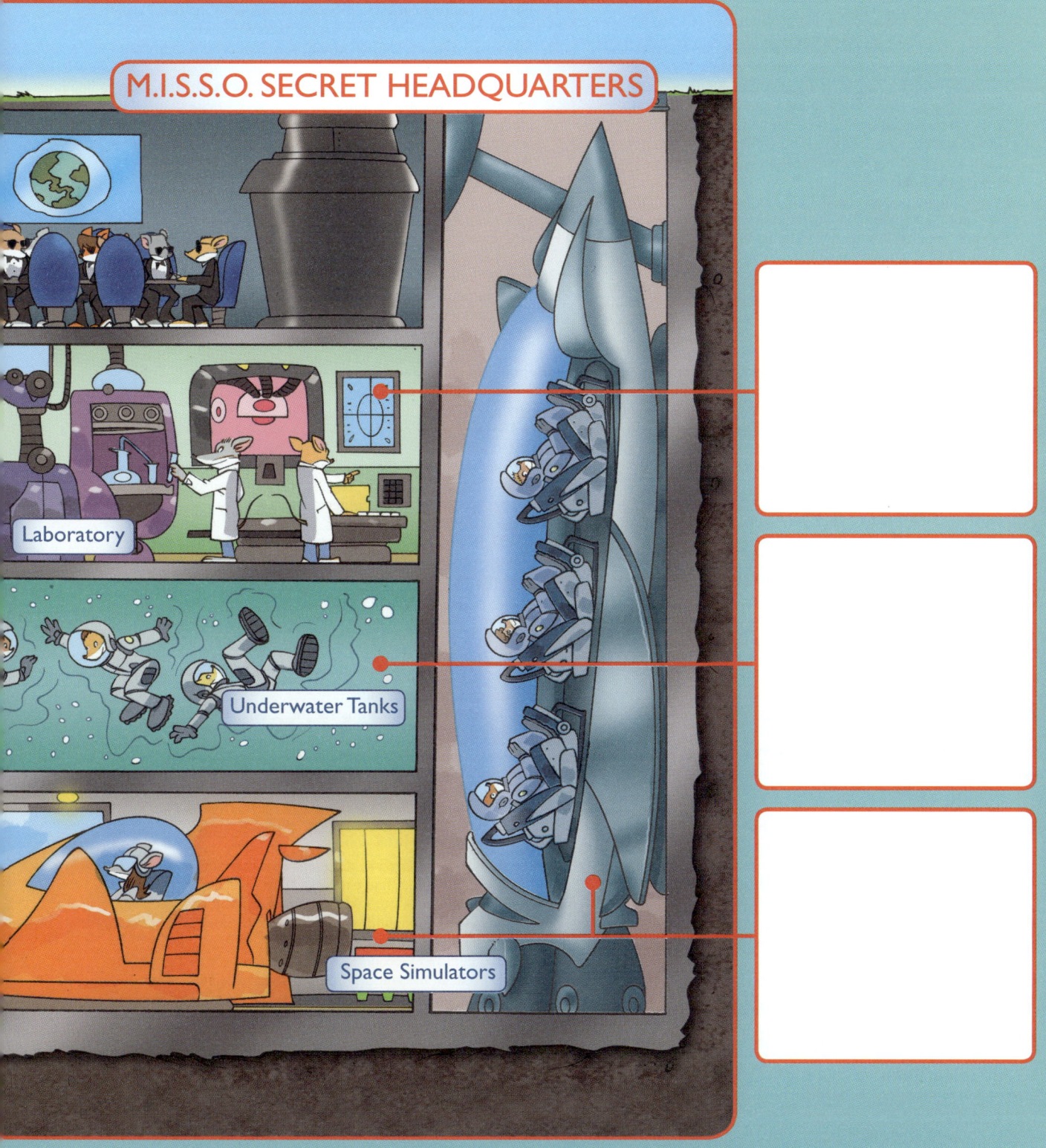

M.I.S.S.O. SECRET HEADQUARTERS

Laboratory

Underwater Tanks

Space Simulators

Excerpt from Mouse in Space!
(Originally published in Italy by Edizioni Piemme S.O.S. C'e un topo nello spazio!)

Answers

Section 1
Unit 1
Pages 6–7
Whilst-reading questions:
1. They have known each other for a long time.
2. They were warm and caring mice.
3. The ghost that has been wandering around the hotel has chased all his guests away and his business has suffered.
4. He thought it was a bad joke.

Page 8
1. He suspected that there might be a connection between the ghost and someone wanting to buy the hotel.
2. He used the word "flush" to suggest that someone wanted to chase them out, but "flush" is also related to toilets and the new owner wanted to build a toilet factory.
3. He was upset and unwilling. He felt that he was being forced to sell it and did not like what Bradley Bigbottom intends to do with the hotel.
4. Event 1: A mysterious rodent has been asking Horatzio to sell the hotel.
   Event 2: A ghost has been wandering around the hotel.
   Event 3: All the guests have been complaining.
   Suggested answer: All three events are related. The mysterious rodent could be responsible for the ghost's appearance and the guests complaining.

Page 9
It was <u>founded</u> by Everest and Arabella Hoteltail. He was a <u>bricklayer</u> and she was a <u>cook</u>. They were poor but <u>full of energy and enthusiasm</u>. He <u>built the hotel</u>, brick by brick. They loved to make travelers happy by letting them <u>enjoy hot meals and comfortable beds</u>. Many guests also came to taste <u>Arabella's delicious dishes</u>. Over the years, the hotel grew and became <u>the most famous hotel in Mouse Island</u>.

Unit 2
Pages 10–11
Whilst-reading questions:
1. They hoped to find out more about the ghost.
2. Matilda Broommouse
3. So that Horatzio would not think that she was not doing her job.
4. The word "seems" suggests that Geronimo did not believe there was a ghost.

Page 12
1. They have quit and left the hotel.
2. He thought that the hotel would have to be shut down.
3. He loves the hotel and calls it a "precious landmark" and the "heart of the city".
4. She was concerned about losing her job.
5. a. That guests have been finding white fur in their soup although no one at the hotel has white hair.
   b. That he has been finding chocolate wrappers in the kitchen although no one there eats chocolates.

Page 13
Appearance:
a. in the dark
b. big and tall
c. creepy clanking armor and chains

Strange Happenings in the Hotel:
a. Spiderwebs
b. white fur in their soup
c. chocolate wrappers in the kitchen

Accept all reasonable answers.

Unit 3
Pages 14–15
Whilst-reading questions:
1. The guests have all left the hotel.
2. A clue to the mystery of the ghost
3. He disliked it a lot.
4. She did not want Geronimo to hear what she was saying.

Page 16
1. He kept hearing eerie violin music throughout the hotel even though the hotel is not wired with a stereo system.
2. Suggested answer: He hoped that someone would figure out what was going on so that the hotel could be saved.
3. No, because he believes that they would "unmask" the ghost and uncover the mastermind.
4. He hoped that he might finally have something to do and help the guests.
5. He noticed that it glowed in the dark and thought that it might belong to the ghost.

Page 17
Physical appearance: tall and stout, dressed beautifully in an elegant black suit, wore a lot of jewelry, wore expensive perfume
Office décor: elegant office with many precious objects, antique furniture, famous paintings
What she said: nothing lasts forever; could easily find another job, has many options

Accept all reasonable answers.

Activity 1
Pages 18–19
Suggested answer:
Deduction: The ghost's glow-in-the-dark appearance was likely from glow-in-the-dark paint. The ghost used the air-conditioning duct to get around, and left spiderwebs all over the place and chocolate wrappers in the kitchen. The white fur in the guests' soup came from the wig and the creepy armor the chef saw was the armor costume and plastic chains. The eerie violin music was from the portable stereo.

Section 2
Unit 4
Pages 20–21
Whilst-reading questions:
1. He doesn't really like Bugsy.
2. No, because she did not answer the phone.
3. He heard that Geronimo was a publisher and knew that he could take advantage of that.
4. Suggested answer: No, because the Bay of Whales had already changed completely and when Geronimo called the hotel, the person working there was very different.

Page 22
1. It means to be amazed to the point that you can't say anything. Geronimo had expected Miss Sweetcakes to answer the phone and was stunned to hear a gruff voice.
2. Yes, because he demanded that Geronimo state his request quickly as he didn't have time to wait.
3. He assumed that Geronimo was rich since he was a publisher.
4. It was because the amount asked for was extremely high.
5. He did not want to look like a cheapskate in front of Petunia.

Page 23
Now, it was a <u>smelly dump</u>. Instead of a pristine coastline, <u>ugly gray buildings</u> crowded the coastline. The once clean beach was now <u>littered with papers and garbage</u>. There used to be no cars but now <u>there were many cars!</u> The air that was once clean and fresh was so polluted because there were <u>many factories spewing smoke into the air</u>.

© 2015 Scholastic Education International (S) Pte Ltd ISBN 978-981-4629-65-2

Unit 5
Pages 24–25
Whilst-reading questions:
1. It was because overeating can make one feel more seasick when one gets on the boat.
2. He is going to get seasick.
3. Petunia may have had a questioning look or a confused look.
4. No, because of the noise from the boat's engine.

Page 26
1. It allowed you to see the fish as if you were right in the water.
2. He thought it was because he was excited about telling Petunia that he liked her.
3. His head spun, his fur turned green, his stomach lurched, his tongue hung out and he shook like a leaf.
4. He probably threw up.
5. Do not eat too much before a boat ride.

Page 27
The day started out with a beautiful view of the sea. It started to get <u>rocky</u> and <u>wobbly</u> and I felt myself feeling a little <u>weird</u>. I regretted <u>eating so much</u>. My stomach <u>hurt</u>. I tried to lie down hoping I would feel better, but then I started to get <u>dizzy</u>. I raced to the edge of the boat…

Geronimo threw up over the side of the boat.

Unit 6
Pages 28–29
Whilst-reading questions:
1. Accept all reasonable answers.
2. No, because whales are usually found in the sea.
3. The whale's skin was getting too dry and it was slowly dying.
4. This was rare because whales normally have a color to their skin and this one did not.

Page 30
1. It might be sick or it might have lost its sense of direction.
2. He realized that the whale's delicate skin needed to be kept moist but as it was on the beach, its skin was drying out.
3. It closed its eyes and stopped spraying water.
4. They only realized it when a moonbeam lit up the whale, as it was in the dark until then.
5. Accept all reasonable answers.

Page 31
What to do: 1, 2, 3 and 4
What not to do: 1, 2, 3, 4, 5 and 6
Students should delete the rest of the options.

Activity 2
Pages 32–33
1. a   2. b   3. b   4. c
Accept all reasonable answers.

Section 3
Unit 7
Pages 34–35
Whilst-reading questions:
1. Trap snored like a train engine.
2. Suggested answers: Trap is a forgetful mouse. / Trap is an irresponsible mouse.

Page 36
1. The three problems were: (i) Grandfather made him go to Sedona to search for the Red Bandit and they didn't know where he was exactly; (ii) Trap went with him; (iii) he had to bring an huge jar of chocolate cheese delight.
2. A bandit refers to someone who is a robber or an outlaw and is considered a bad guy.

3. He wanted to eat the chocolate spread.
4. What Geronimo expected:
   • That it had few inhabitants
   • That it had a mild climate

   What he really experienced:
   • Sedona was now a city with more than 10,000 inhabitants.
   • Sedona was extremely hot when they went there.

Page 37
i) He tried to shade it with a huge patio umbrella.
ii) He tried to cool it down by fanning it.
iii) He tried putting ice cubes on the lid to stop it from melting.

Unit 8
Page 38–39
Whilst-reading questions:
1. She expected him to have found the Red Bandit.
2. It was very hot.
3. He was trying to say, "What is it?".
4. It is likely to be filled with many problems.

Page 40
1. He was probably going on a hiking trip.
2.

Experience	Trap	Geronimo
Lodging	• four-star hotel	• none • walking across the desert
Comfort	• very soft bed • tub with massage jets	• slept on doormat • painful experience in the desert
Meal	• delicious cheese soufflé • cheese omelet	• no breakfast

3. He wanted to keep an eye on Grandfather's new hat. No, he probably wanted to continue enjoying his stay at the hotel.
4. Accept all reasonable answers.

Page 41
First, I had to <u>rappel down a mountain</u>. Then the horse I was riding bucked and reared and threw <u>me off its back</u>.
Next, I landed on a cactus and was <u>pricked by cactus spikes</u>. That really hurt! I leaped out of the cactus patch and landed <u>in puma poo</u>. Yuck!
Just when I thought things couldn't get any worse, I narrowly missed <u>a rattlesnake</u>, <u>scorpion</u>, and a <u>tarantula</u>.
I <u>blistered my paws</u> walking across the desert through the night.

Unit 9
Pages 42–43
Whilst-reading questions:
1. He said that so that Geronimo would not give up.
2. It was the Red Bandit.
3. From an old photograph
4. Suggested answer: It was very homely.

Page 44
1. He struggled under the weight of the enormous jar and also because the currents were very strong.
2. The Red Bandit did not have a phone or electricity.
3. He meant that he had many stories to share with Geronimo.
4. Suggested answer:
   • Friendly: he saved Geronimo and took care of him
   • Observant: he recognized Geronimo straightaway
   • Contented: he built his own cabin; does not need a lot to be happy
   • Nature-lover: he only wanted to be in touch with nature and to protect it

Page 45
- a fireplace brightened by a warm, crackling fire; small window; log cabin made out of wood; quilt handmade out of colorful fabric squares; cozy bed
- Accept all reasonable answers.

Activity 2
Pages 46–47
Suggested answer:

About Sedona Arizona:
- Sedona lies in the Verdant Valley of Arizona. The town was named after the wife of one of the settlers.
- Sedona is one of the biggest tourist attractions in the state and it has natural beauty, a mild climate with lots of sunshine.

Attractions Around Sedona:
- Sandstone formations known as red rocks, the most impressive being Cathedral Rock.
- The Grand Canyon, an immense gorge that is many miles long and wide and 1 mile deep, and was carved by the Colorado River. It is one of the major national parks in the United States.

Activities in Sedona:
Visitors can enjoy outdoor activities like hiking, biking, golf, tennis, horseback riding and excursions in helicopters or hot-air balloons. They can also do rappelling and white-water rafting.

Section 4
Unit 10
Pages 48–49
Whilst-reading questions:
1. He probably hit his head on something.
2. He cared more about his pet and things of sentimental value than about his money.
3. It was odd that the intruders did not take his money.
4. He found it hard to believe that Geronimo had managed to chase the burglars away with just a slipper.

Page 50
1. He had a lump on his head and wanted to make sure that he was still thinking properly.
2. They did not steal anything.
3. He was proud of himself. He called himself "a true hero".
4. He wanted his Grandfather to be proud of him.
5. Grandfather is not convinced that Geronimo was a hero. This can be seen from his snort and what he ordered Geronimo to do.

Page 51
1. Stronger   2. Prouder   3. Heroic

Image B.
1. Geronimo called himself the biggest scaredy-mouse on all of Mouse Island.
2. He wanted to boast about how he scared the robbers away.
3. Grandfather snorted in disbelief when he told him about his adventures.
4. Grandfather thought he was making up stories.

Unit 11
Pages 52–53
Whilst-reading questions:
1. Suggested answer: No, because her appearance looked mysterious and her surname "Slyrat" sounded suspicious.
2. He seemed to be hypnotized.
3. Accept all reasonable answers.
4. Accept all reasonable answers.

Page 54
1. Geronimo hadn't even finished his call when a company representative was at the door.
2. She seems suspicious because she was wearing "mysterious black sunglasses". This is reinforced by her name which suggests that she was a sly rat.
3. She did not want him to change his mind or read anything else in the contract.
4. This stands for 24 hours a day, 7 days a week and is a way of saying, all the time.
5. • "I can already tell you are supersmart mouse".
   • "No thieves will get into your house again."
   • "you will receive three pieces of equipment for the price of two!"

Page 55
1) Track movement
2) To sense the presence of living things in the building
3) Record everything that happens everywhere
4) Sense vibrations near the entrance
5) Reliable and shatterproof to prevent entry through windows
6) So loud it can be heard miles away

Unit 12
Pages 56–57
Whilst-reading questions:
1. This suggested that he was unfit and not suited to be an astronaut.
2. He was hoping to run away and not be an astronaut.
3. No, because he was hoping to avoid going into space.
4. Suggested answer: He was probably shocked or in a daze.

Page 58
1. They had already been through training.
2. It was to determine how physically fit Geronimo was.
3. He was happy to find that he might have an excuse not to be an astronaut.
4. No, the professor could tell that he was in bad physical shape, he did not have a degree in Science, and he was obviously afraid of everything.
5. Accept all reasonable answers.

Page 59
1. Pool Training. The 12 hours of training in the pool with full gear with space suit is to help teach him how to move in space.

2. Zero-Gravity Training On a Parabolic Flight. The 12 hours of parabolic flight is to teach him to get used to the lack of gravity.

3. Simulating Flight. The 8 hours of simulated aerospace piloting is to teach him how to steer a spaceship.

Activity 4
Pages 60–61
- Meeting Room: Where management meets to discuss plans and make important decisions
- Medical Examination Room: Where doctors check astronauts to see if they are well and fit
- Control Room: Where they control the flights and tell astronauts what to do
- Laundry Room: Where all the clothing gets washed
- Laboratory: Where scientists do their testing and research
- Underwater Tanks: Where astronauts train with their space suits
- Space Simulators: Where astronauts learn to pilot the spaceships

© 2015 Scholastic Education International (S) Pte Ltd ISBN 978-981-4629-65-2